THE GREATEST TEAMMATE

Making Jesus Your Number 1 Draft Choice

DAVID L. ANGERON
M.S., CSPC

Copyright© 2021 David Angeron. All rights reserved
Published by:
John Melvin Publishing, LLC
344 St. Joseph St.
Suite 538
New Orleans, LA 70130
www.johnmelvinpublishing.com
ISBN: 978-1-7369768-2-1 (Paperback)
ISBN: 978-1-7369768-3-8 (Hardback)
Library of Congress Control Number: 2021907793

No part of this work may be reproduced or transmitted in any form or by any means, electronic, manual, photocopying, recording, or by any information storage and retrieval system, without prior written permission of the publisher.

Printed in the United States of America

Table of Contents

INTRODUCTION: HOW TO USE THIS BOOK 1

CHAPTER 1: STARTING OVER 13

CHAPTER 2: ADVERSITY & RESILIENCE 31

CHAPTER 3: UNDERDOG 45

CHAPTER 4: FACED WITH DOUBT 61

CHAPTER 5: OVERCOMING FEAR 75

CHAPTER 6: COMMITMENT & MOTIVATION 89

CHAPTER 7: GOALS AND GOD'S WILL 105

CHAPTER 8: PRAYER AND IMAGERY 121

CHAPTER 9: CONFIDENCE 135

CHAPTER 10: THE GREATEST TEAMMATE 151

CHAPTER 11: GOOD LIFE: LOSING EVERYTHING & FOUND EVERYTHING 167

ACKNOWLEDGMENTS 183

REFERENCES 187

Introduction

HOW TO USE THIS BOOK

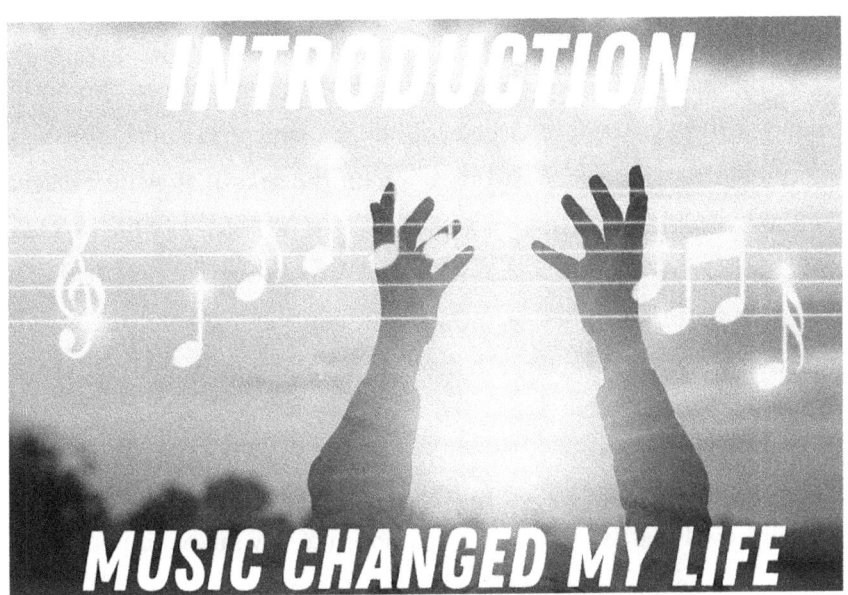

B efore we start, allow me to briefly introduce myself to you. I was raised in a Christian family and members of a Baptist church in the small town of Bayou Vista, Louisiana. My mom would make us go to Sunday school and church service every Sunday.

She would come into my room at night and make me say my prayers before I went to sleep each night. It was not a burden, I actually enjoyed church and hanging out with friends in our youth group. I enjoyed playing sports in our youth church league on weekends. I remember reading my bible as a child but only to look up verses we had to memorize for Sunday school. As I entered high school, my mom stopped coming into my room to say my prayers, but she would come in to tell me good night and say, "Remember to say your prayers." Most nights I would say them on my own. Growing up, I remember a lot about church, and I knew the basics about God and the Bible, but that was mainly because I had to go to church with my family.

When I got older and moved onto college and the real-world work force, the habits of going to church and praying started to slip away from me. I was a college athlete, so all my time and dedication was spent focusing on practice and studying for the next final. After college, I started coaching high school sports and got married. My life seemed to be doing fine and on a smooth path. A few years later we had our first 2 children, and they were my pride and joy. But my focus and priorities were still on the game that I loved and my coaching career.

When my son turned 3 years old and my daughter was an infant, I received an offer for my first professional baseball job—my dream job. That is how I ended up in Pensacola, Florida. My salary doubled, and I lived in a penthouse condo on beautiful Pensacola Beach. Not even sure that I deserved this opportunity, but it felt as though I must have been living right. Five years into my professional coaching career, church and prayer was the last thing on my mind. I lived a life that most people could only dream about. I had an impressive place to live, drove a Hummer, and received VIP treatment at every local restaurant and club in town. But here I was, with all of those material things, and I was depressed and miserable. I realized my priorities were messed up, my marriage was failing, I was on the road all the time losing precious moments with my children, and I never went to visit my parents or any other family. Baseball was all I cared about at the time. I knew I needed to change my priorities, but I did not know how. I continued coaching for one more season and ended up divorced. Unsure what direction or path I was supposed to follow, I felt totally lost. I ended up going to counseling, trying to save my marriage. I did everything I thought would help, but was still depressed and spiraling down. I could not seem to find the answers to make things better. So, I prayed about it. I could not tell you the last time I took the time to pray, but I was desperate. I did not know where else to turn.

That summer I worked at a youth baseball camp for kids between eight to twelve years old. At the end of the day, the kids were talking about the MLB baseball draft and who their favorite players were. So, I asked them if they could pick any player to be their number one draft pick, whom would they choose? At first, they all started blurting out names. I remember hearing Mickey Mantle, Barry Bonds, Mark McGuire. Then, I made them all stop and raise their hand to share their number one draft choice. The first person I called on said, "Pete Rose", then the next kid said, "Ken Griffey Jr.", then "Babe Ruth", and so on. I was about to stop calling on kids when I saw one of the shy little eight-year-olds in the back with his hand up. I remember his name was Jonathon. When I asked Jonathon who his number one draft choice would be, he looked at me with big brown eyes and said, "Coach, I would pick God first." The other kids started laughing, and I immediately stopped them. I looked at Jonathan and told him that was the best answer I had heard. I even gave him one of our door prizes, a bat bag, since he was brave enough to say that answer out loud.

The Greatest Teammate

As I went home that night, I prayed again for direction and answers of how to turn my life around. That is when it hit me. I heard the answer I was looking for from an eight-year-old at baseball camp earlier that day. I have always been a "Christian". I believed in God, went to church, and I would pray. But I never had a *true relationship* with God. I could honestly say, I never had God as a teammate. I turned to God when I was younger because my parents made me, and I would turn to him as I got older because I needed something. I never made God my priority until that summer day. From that day on, I vowed to make God my number one draft choice in everything I do. And from that day forward, my life began to change. I realized all the blessings I had in my life. My depression vanished.

I changed my priority—once all about baseball—to what I live by today: G.F.E.B (God, Family, Education, and Baseball).

This book is intended to draw our heart and mind towards the verses of the Bible and asks us to pay attention. Pay attention to what? Pay attention to what we're seeking. Is it outside of us or within us? Is it success? If it is, then, what are the ways we have employed for that success? How truthful are we about that success? Have we got any life left in us or around us after achieving that success? The Bible speaks eloquently to us, "May he grant you your heart's desire and fulfill all your plans" (*ESV*, Psalm 20:4). Yes, we should desire, but carefully. So, is it the mind which will take us to what we desire? Then, we must feel joy and pleasure in working towards it. For, it wouldn't be intelligent of us to labor for something that doesn't bear any joy. Yes, we can achieve anything by our faith and faith alone if our desires are real. The Lord says, "Knock and the door will be opened to you" (*NIV*, Matthew 7:7). Then the light of spirit will lighten our mind.

David L. Angeron

It is incumbent on us to pay attention to the verse "For those who are led by the spirit of God are the children of god" (*NIV,* Romans 8:14). In that sense we all share a common human spirit, distinct in its own way on an individual level. So we must strive towards understanding what this spirituality is all about—which many of us have abandoned in the already isolated world. How can we relate the wisdom of the Bible to the profession we pursue for a more fulfilling life? Also, how can it relate to our sports teams?

We will talk in detail about the references by recalling examples in the latter part of the book. The Bible is not only the basis of a Christian's life, but it has also inspired a whole culture of writers, artists, athletes, performers, musicians, and entrepreneurs.

There was a long tradition of interspersing Biblical passages with arias, choruses, and hymns. Music was regularly arranged on Biblical passages. Church music has always been part of the Christian aesthetics, as a form of prayer. We sing Carols during Christmas. Singing elevates our senses. It symbolizes the beauty of Christian life, as we sing in praise of Christ. Here, singing takes a social, as well as an individual form. It binds us to a community, as well as it connects us to our being. We will discuss one or two verses of music when we start introducing the chapters of the book.

If someone asks us what Christian spirituality is all about, our answer would be that it's the intimate loving relationship between God's Holy Spirit and the spirit of believers. Hence, we say, 'Our Father' and not 'My father' or 'Your Father', because it relates to the human spirit in all of us. It reminds us that we are one commune. We're not alone. It includes our social, political, family, sexual, and economic lives. It reminds believers of the suffering of Christ to deliver humans of its evil and put the word suffering at the core of Christian spirituality. We must recognize the pain in order to sail over it, so that we could reconcile with God. We must recall the Bible verse which says, "All this is from God, who reconciled us to himself through Christ and gave us the ministry of reconciliation: that God was reconciling the world to himself in Christ, not counting people's sins against them. And he has committed to us the message of reconciliation. We are therefore Christ's ambassadors, as though God were making his appeal through us. We implore you on Christ's behalf: Be reconciled to God" (*NIV*, 2 Corinthians 5:18-20).

This book is an attempt to bring the unvarnished truth of life in its unadorned form to its readers. To bring them closer to God, while discussing different travails and trials like fear, adversity, and doubt one's face through their sporting lives or life in general. The parables of Jesus are a treasure trove of knowledge which this book would share with the readers to further fortify the reader's approach to life in general and excel in their lives by just incorporating the beautiful values of the Bible into their sports.

When I first started thinking about writing this book, it took me a while to decide on themes that best relate to the chapters and would really connect with the readers. I prayed for guidance on the best way to bring this book together. Each chapter in my previous book, *The Mental Training Guide For Elite Athletes*, was written based on themes from inspirational quotes. However, for this book I wanted something different. Something that could make each reader feel a connection with the passion of Christ in his or her soul. One morning I was running a 5k race and listening to my running mix on my headphones.

When I got about halfway through the race—it hit me. My music doesn't just motivate me to exercise and get through races; it also motivates me to focus on living a quality Christian life. It was music that redirected me back to my connection with Jesus. That's when I used some of my favorite songs from my Christian running mix as the themes of each chapter. I strongly encourage you to listen to each song before and after each chapter so you can truly feel the connection. Here is a brief description of the forthcoming chapters, themes, and songs to look forward to.

The first chapter discusses our capacity to start over after light eludes us and we hit the abyss—when failure defines our being. People cast aspersions on us and we keep fondling in the dark. We come to a breaking point where even the essence of God vanishes from our lives. A kind of horror submerges the soul that whether we would make it out of here. There's no love. In the absence of love, the soul also stops seeking. But if we persist and go beyond just hoping a light would emerge. The hand of God reaches out to us. Then we start over. Music is a form of praise to God. It raises your soul towards God. The theme of the first chapter is from the song "Start Over" by *Flame*. Listen to the song and feel the world dissolve around you and let it transcend you towards the gate of heaven, and feel the spirit of Jesus.

The second chapter explains the point of resilience in the time of adversity. Being resilient means we persist and not waver. We endure for a long time without buckling under its pressure. It is the firmness of will in the face of failure. Even in good times we don't give in to the pleasure of prodigality, or flesh. We endure life with the virtues of faith, hope, and charity. It's a lifelong commitment towards the grace of God that we would be sustained in good until the end of our time.

Whenever our will falters, we should pray while listening to the song "Praise you in this Storm" by *Casting Crowns*.

The third chapter belongs to an underdog who bides his time with his unwavering belief. David and Goliath is one such story. The ideal of our country champions an underdog who despite all the odds rises. He fights the injustice and comes back stronger when a rich man rigs the last game. While the underdog in us prepares to humble our opponent, we can give some respite to our bruised soul by listening to "Underdog" by *Audio Adrenaline*.

The fourth chapter deals with what we should do when faced with doubt. Doubt creeps in when there is a lack of belief in ourselves. Doubt cripples us. It's like being tied to a stone and thrown into the river. The more we struggle with it, the more we drown. We suspend our faculty of judgment when in doubt. The more we doubt, the more it hampers the quality of our judgment. We are going to investigate this debilitating emotion in us where we become indecisive and uncertainty looms large. For the one who doubts, is like a wave of the sea that is driven and tossed into the wind says the Bible (*ESV,* James 1:6). "Voice of Truth" by *Casting Crowns* is the theme of the chapter. Truth is what we need, when our mind struggles with the falsity triggered by our doubt.

The fifth chapter teaches us the way out of our fear. Fear is such a strong emotion that it freezes our thoughts and seriously compromises the independence of our mind. Fear takes us away from the awareness of our 'self'. Courage brings us closer to the realization of our 'self'. We will discuss the types of courage in this chapter. For example, the passive courage we show in the face of tyranny. We will discuss the kind of courage where we are calm and composed in the face of a storm. The theme of this chapter is from the song, "Courageous" by *Casting Crowns*.

The sixth chapter is about commitment and motivation. We should inspect what the leading desire is for the motivated soul. Now in an animal, the desire for nutrition or food motivates a motion in them. We are also an animal, but with the agency of a thinking mind. Please add the capacity of imagination to it as well. So, our desire varies. It's a possibility that we could be led by a sinful desire. Hence keep the Bible as your guide which says, "Now the works of the flesh are evident: sexual immorality, impurity, sensuality, idolatry, sorcery, enmity, strife, jealousy, fits of anger, rivalries, dissensions, divisions, envy, drunkenness, orgies, and things like these. I warn you, as I warned you before, that those who do such things will not inherit the kingdom of God" (*ESV,* Galatians 5:19-21). We have to keep our motivation where the spirit of God desires us to be. "God is Enough" by *Lecrae* is the theme of this chapter. True motivation can be found in this song.

The seventh chapter discusses the reason for our motivation—which is a goal. The immediate goal we achieve, to survive our earthly lives, towards an ultimate goal, which harmonizes us with the will of God. Goals are important. We must know where we are headed—on an individual level as well as a community level. We will discuss the will of God and all its aspects in this chapter. Such as—whether there is a will in God, whether God wills things apart from himself, and whether the divine will is always fulfilled. After understanding the will of God, we will work towards our goal. Of course our goal has an end. Does this end have the aspects of good? If it's not, then what must be done to make our end good? Meanwhile, we listen to "Move" by *Flame*—which is the theme of this chapter.

The eighth chapter discusses prayer and imagery. Prayer is the expression of our love towards God. It's the expression of our profound affection. It flows from the interiors of our heart and manifests outside and reveals an understanding of what we are as a human being. "Our Father" is the most perfect prayer. It is brief, perfect, and effective. It teaches us everything that we may ask from God. We must remain careful here of what we desire. Prayer therefore teaches us not only how to ask, what to ask, it also teaches us to remain affectionate, humble, and confident before God. To speak of human beings as the image of God necessarily represents the exemplary that is the face of Christ. The human race imitates Christ's face because he is the perfect image of the father. We will discuss elaborately about prayer and its aesthetics in a Christian life in this chapter. The theme of this chapter is Imagery and Prayer. It is a song called "I can only Image" by *Mercy Me*.

The ninth chapter discusses confidence because God asks us that we will be confident and we will not fear (*GW*, Isaiah 12:2). Confidence is opposed to fear. And we will be rewarded thus. Confidence takes its name from 'fides' (faith): faith brings hope. A man shows confidence when he hopes to get help from the one who promises to help him—God. A man also shows confidence in the hope of having something. He could have health. He could be powerful. Confidence is the way through which a man shows his strength of hope that he will achieve a certain good. Confidence also arises from opinion. How meritorious are we? Will we get commendation? Will we get affection? We will discuss the virtue of being confident in this chapter. It's important to be confident in ourselves and also show the same amount of confidence in others. We must feel some power within ourselves, even if we feel we're less able than others.

"You can't stop me" by *Andy Mineo* is the theme of this chapter. We take encouragement from the verses of this song and keep moving.

The tenth chapter brings us to face the ultimate truth that the truest ally we have is God. In this chapter we inquire about the presence of God.

If we direct our desire towards the will of God and make it one of the most indispensable parts of our spiritual lives—for only God has the power to raise our soul. He would certainly come to those who will seek him. God will become our greatest teammate. How? We will explore this further in the next chapter. The theme of this chapter is "Awesome God" by *R. Swift*. We must bring this song closer to our heart.

Finally, in the eleventh chapter, we will discuss what a good life truly is—a life that is worthwhile. For that kind of life, we must recognize the necessities through which we will go about our lives. We must understand we're specks in the larger scheme of things. And nature is immensely powerful. How do we align with nature and not change it according to our will to achieve what we desire in our lives? We must introspect on what is at stake and prioritize accordingly. Are we employing our energy in the right direction? Is there any method to our directed energy? The truth is, we must adapt. We must harmonize ourselves with nature. Only after adapting ourselves, we pursue our passions. It lies in the way through which we apply our efforts—the conditioning of our necessities in order to realize our passions. That is how we will have a worthwhile life. Now if greed takes over, and the ephemeral power we think has led us towards the destruction of balance with nature—we then must recall the Parable of Prodigal Son. In this parable, a son wastes everything given to him by his father in his extravagant life. He returns a pauper when better sense prevails. The father doesn't judge him and accepts him. If you ask for bread from your father, he will not give you stone. We will discuss the parable and also what this good life entails in this chapter. Meanwhile, we can satisfy our soul with the song, "Good Life" by *Audio Adrenaline*.

The sole ambition of this book is to bring the Christian spirituality through the aesthetics, beauty, and wisdom of the Bible into the lives of the readers. And try to embrace the spirit of the readers with a larger whole, which is the spirit of God where they could humbly face the pitfalls of life and follow their passion with renewed strength. Can we absorb the Bible's essence in the sporting lives of the Athletes? Yes, we can. And it's a humble attempt to bring you closer to my *Greatest Teammate*.

David L. Angeron

www.davidangeron.com

Chapter 1
STARTING OVER

"START OVER"–BY FLAME

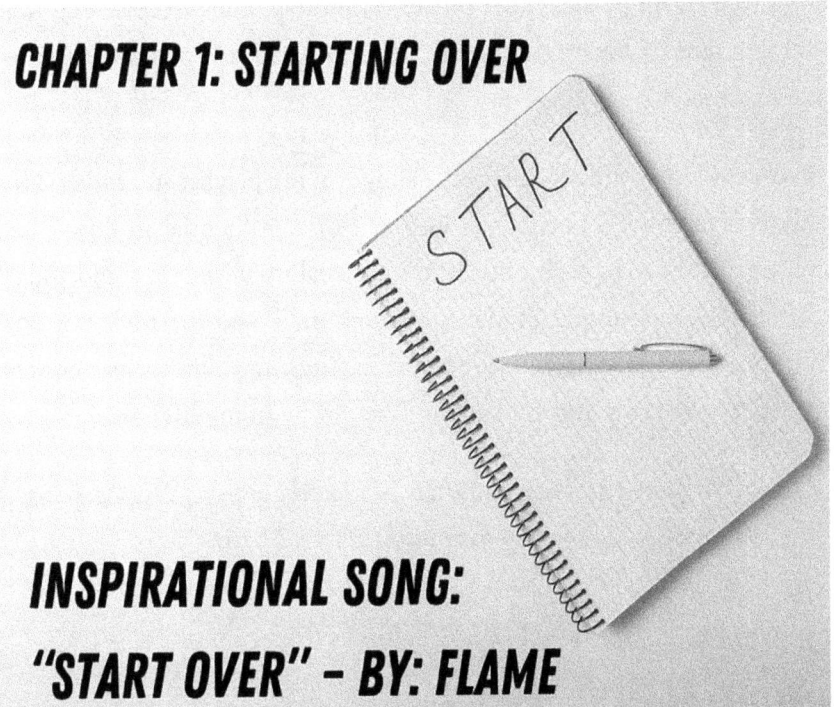

CHAPTER 1: STARTING OVER

**INSPIRATIONAL SONG:
"START OVER" - BY: FLAME**

If you read the introduction to this book, then you will know that my life was, at one time, completely unraveled. I am not saying music is the "saving grace" for everyone, but it was this Christian music playlist that I mention in each chapter that helped me recognize that I needed to stop and reconnect with God. For a few years, I was completely lost, depressed, and completely out of shape. I made a commitment to get back into physical shape. One day as I was running, my shoe had untied, so I immediately stopped to retie it. At that moment, with my iPod on shuffle mode, a song in my running mix called "Start Over" by Flame began playing. The song immediately gripped me. It made me realize that for the last few years, my life was unraveling just like my shoelace. But instead of stopping to retie it and starting over, I just kept running and tripping on life's challenges. I did not instantly pop back into peace, happiness, and success, but that moment and that song started my work to reconnect with my number one teammate.

Start Over is one of my favorite songs on my playlist still today. Not only is it extremely fitting, but also it is also influential in how I live my life and how I coach others that are dealing with stress and tough times. As I mentioned in the introduction, I had hit rock bottom. Without reconnecting with God and having the ability to be resilient and start over, I am not sure where I would be in my life today.

Jesus, He gave it all to save you/ He carried the cross on His shoulders
So you can start over (Flame, 2013).

David L. Angeron

We must not forget at each moment of our existence is God's love for us. God's mercy is manifested in affliction as in joy. But what do we have to offer? We have a soul to offer to God and a blank piece of paper to rewrite our own story and take control of our own lives by existing every day in the grace of God.

Your parents brought you up the best they could, and with what they had, good or bad. Maybe you're still living with them and are already looking forward to making it on your own. Wherever you're at, God will meet you there.

Oftentimes it's hard to imagine having a clean slate—that blank piece of paper where you feel everything great in life is possible and you can dream of that baseball career or maybe a career in coaching. The paper we often look at is filled with heavy responsibilities, failures we can't forget, labels people have placed upon us, opportunities missed or people and circumstances that seem immoveable.

Nothing seems more horrible and immoveable than your last mistake and the people that won't let you forget it.

God forgives. God gives us humans the gift of resilience. No matter if you hit rock bottom, you have the ability to bounce back. Jesus assures his compassion through simple truths.

Jesus is the mediator—through him you can access the grace of God. Thomas Aquinas writes that through grace, we are helped by him to do right; we must consider the grace of God. The material sun sheds its light outside us, but the intelligible sun, who is God, shines inside us (P.2528). Hence the light which falls on the soul is God's light. You can always come back. It just takes a willing heart ready to listen, a plan, discipline and staying focused.

It's easy to stay focused when you have your priorities set, and in this book you'll learn what your priorities are and how to stay focused on them—the way I did in order to get myself out of my own slump. I created G.F.E.B, but yours might be different because we all have different lives, different goals and unique traits and talents. This book is about how to find yours.

I am not saying it's easy to make the 180-degree turn from where you are now and completely change your way of living, but this book will guide you through attainable steps to help you bounce back and live a happy life with God as your greatest teammate.

No matter where you are, what you've gone through or have done, God is there and you can start again, this time, with all faith that all good comes to those who love God and make Him the priority. When you make this choice to give up the old ways; the habits that waste time and get you in trouble, the old thinking that beats you down and makes it tough to show up and give your absolute best performance, you'll see on the other side of those choices is a life of freedom and power—a confidence no one can touch.

To do this, you need to consider the mental side of your game, and the mental side of life. Those thoughts in your head that quietly say, "Hey, man, it's all good if you skip your workout today. Just tell the coach you did it, no one will know" or the thought, "You screw that up every time you're at bat, you'll never get it right." These thoughts are under your control because God gave you the power to replace them, demolish them, and better yet, replace them with the truth. The truth is, you are created in God's image and likeness. Jesus commanded his followers to do more, and do better, than even he did—healing the sick and casting out demons. Though the Bible uses old language and stories that may not seem as relevant today with our phones and computers and cars, we can take those stories in the Bible and match them to our current lives and realize we have the power to heal our lives. This is done by accepting God as our number one teammate; allowing God into our hearts and minds and letting Him guide us through all the inevitable hard times that come up.

GAUGE WHERE YOU ARE, SO YOU KNOW WHERE YOU'RE HEADED.

Where are you right now? Do you know how well you're really doing? Has the coach stopped talking to you? Are your teammates your friends? Are people telling you that you're doing better than you are, and you know there's something off? Do you want more out of your sports career, but it just seems too far away to grab? How are your personal relationships? Is there fighting and struggling? Difficulty communicating and being heard?

I've used this formula for assessing my player's position and how to gauge how they're really doing both in sports and life, and I think you'll find it helpful.

Answer the following questions and go ahead and write your answers down in the book. Circle the ones that are most like you:

Sports Life

1. After our team wins, I'm usually the one everyone is congratulating and I've got a lot of pull with the coach. It makes me feel like a fraud sometimes, like it's too easy and I don't feel challenged enough. I might be good in my small town, but I want to hit it big and I don't know what to do next. I just get slaps on the back, not actual guidance.
2. Working hard is what I'm known for, and it fills gaps in talent I wasn't born with. Not being the most talented is tough, and I work harder than others, so that can make me upset sometimes when others are lazy. So I go between feeling down to wanting to punch my teammates.

3. I know exactly where I am right now and where I'm going. I have goals and numbers I must meet, otherwise I get upset and sometimes beat myself up over it. My fighting spirit and competitiveness are all I've got. If people can't handle me, they just leave.
4. I'm just playing because it's fun and I'm pretty good at it. I love hanging with the guys and being part of the team. Where they go, I go. I'm not totally sure what my next move is, and I've not really been engaged with my goals.

Family Life

1. My family is my biggest fan and I can do no wrong in their eyes. It's nice, but there's no challenge and I feel like I have to figure everything out on my own in order to improve.
2. My family loves sports and they tend to coach and critique me after games.
3. My family doesn't really engage much in my sports career.
4. My family is my team, along with those friends I like to hang with.

How You Were Raised

1. I was raised with a super supportive family that was happy with whatever I did and left everything up to me.
2. I was brought up to work hard and not complain so when I see other players with easygoing families I always think that would be nice to have, even though I'm proud of being hardworking.
3. If I don't meet my goals or hit my numbers, my family knows to leave me alone and let me be. I don't need their support.

4. I'd rather be hanging out with my friends than with my family all the time.

Spiritual Life

5. God and going to church is not a practical thing for me on a regular basis, and it's more of a family thing.
6. God and going to church is about doing what you're supposed to be doing because you should.
7. God and going to church is all about family tradition.
8. I wasn't raised in church and don't really connect with God in that way.

My Life Right Now

1. Life is okay. It looks good from the outside, but I'm not happy with what's going on inside. I want more and I want to be better.
2. I don't feel like people entirely understand me and I feel undervalued. I want to be better in everything, yet I also feel overworked.
3. If I want something I go get it, but honestly, I'm not always happy when I get it. I'm missing something and I'd like to know what I could do to get it.
4. I'm usually having a good time no matter what, but if I'm not part of a team or with my friends, I'm honestly directionless. My worst day would be one where I'm entirely alone and nothing is happening. My significant other has to take a backseat to my teammates and my friends sometimes.

JUST OKAY, IS NOT OKAY

Everything might seem okay right now. Life has a way of ebbing and flowing from good times to bad. Often there's a lot of time just coasting along and you think, "Well, everything seems alright enough." This is the perfect time, right now, to start over. Decide before the inevitable downturn. How can you gauge where you're at?

ALL WORK AND NO PLAY

Like it or not, you are a hard worker and most people can't keep up with your work ethic. When you work that hard, it's difficult to take time to really relax and not feel guilty or agitated about not doing anything. It can be a vicious cycle, and what seems like a great attribute of being hardworking, can turn into a habit that causes you to break down; become sick, become intolerant and upset with people that don't match our work ethic, inability to slow down enough to listen to others, let alone God's own direction that comes by way of intuition.

GOD IS THE CENTER OF THE UNIVERSE, NOT YOU

This isn't coming as a shock—you often run your life as though nothing else matters, and no one else matters as much as what you need to accomplish. Hey, your attitude has gotten you this far and you've seen success, so why change anything? But do you have everything you want? Are you fully satisfied in this very moment that you've accomplished everything? How connected are you really to the people around you?

ALL PLAY WILL LEAVE YOU EMPTY

It's like going to fill your gas tank and getting distracted by a conversation with a buddy and only filling your tank part of the way because you didn't notice the pump clicked off too early by accident. Being distracted by the next party, the next adventure, the next gathering of your team so you can goof off and enjoy the camaraderie instead of taking your contribution seriously will do the same—leave you empty.

It leaves your teammates and coach empty because they only have your attention and participation as long as you're having a good time. Soon as it gets rough and the numbers aren't being met, you're standing there with not much to offer.

Normally, I'm about the positive; a positive mindset and a positive outlook. When you make mistakes or reveal something negative about yourself or your performance, it's best to recognize it, find solutions, then focus on implementing the best solution in a positive way. There's no looking backward after you resolve to focus on changing something for the better and put forth the effort to do it.

Starting over after a big loss, recognizing a bad habit, finding yourself at the bottom can seem overwhelming. This is the perfect time to sit down and ask if you can do this alone. Do you want to do it alone, always carrying the burden? What if I told you that God is waiting for you right now to choose Him as your teammate on the field and in life so you don't have to carry those burdens anymore?

What is bothering you today? What's been on your mind and gnawing at you lately? Take a minute and think about what those answers are and write them down.

> *Everybody's got a blank page*
> *A story they're writing today*
> *A wall that they're climbing*
> *You can carry the past on your shoulders*
> *Or you can start over (Flame, 2013).*

Now, take a look at those burdens that cause stress and keep you back from accomplishing your dreams and goals. Are they worth the battle? Are you exhausted playing whack-a-mole with your issues? One pops up, you hit it and it's gone (you think) then another just pops up so you're constantly whacking away at your problems to never see them really go away? The only way to stand back and toss away the club is to let God into your heart, your mind, and be free. And that will not be an irrational act. If we have to believe in Thomas Aquinas' words, we cannot give God anything he has not first given us (P. 377). We have been created rational, and we believe in his providence, which governs us for our good and all the other creatures of this world for the same good. That is how we're united to God by an act of love because we have been addressed personally.

Now is the time to decide for yourself. Who do you want as your teammate? Are you ready to put down your whack-a-mole club and let God guide you through the turmoil of life and the unpredictability of your performance on the field? Are you ready to accept having the most powerful, loving, and perfect teammate a player could ever have?

HOW TO MAKE A DECISION & MAKE IT STICK

You have good intentions when you're getting excited and planning something new. It's fun looking through pictures of the vehicle you'd love to buy when you're making the big money. You get excited, share it with your friends, and maybe even check your credit score and bank account to see how far off you are from purchasing it. You may tape a picture of it on your wall. Then daily life grinds on and you're still climbing into your little Honda Civic, waiting for the day your transmission wears out entirely.

The key here is NOT WAITING until the tranny goes out. Why wait until the point you don't have a car to drive anymore and it's more painful to ask friends to borrow theirs or rent a car, all so you can plop down a bunch of money on a car you don't even like anymore?

Same thing goes for your spiritual life as your inner life. That inner voice talking to you is waiting for another day to work out. What's one more day of taking a break or doing it the same way? Nothing bad has happened yet. Many people that drink alcohol and take other drugs have that same thought. What's the harm in one time? There's nothing wrong with one more time . . .

Your old Honda Civic is there ready to show you that one more day can mean disaster—like you sitting on the side of the road in a downpour waiting for the tow truck. So why not create the easy path forward by taking initiative? When you do this in life (with your car, homework, bills) you lessen the stress, you lessen the time wasted on fixing what's broken or forgotten, and it gives you more time to focus on bettering yourself; improving your physical strength, improving your averages and becoming the best ball player you can.

Acceptance: No matter what our past may have been, God accepts us unconditionally, but He loves us too much to leave us the way we are. *It's in the Bible*, "But if a wicked man turns from all his sins which he has committed, keeps all My statutes, and does what is lawful and right, he shall surely live; he shall not die. None of the transgressions which he has committed shall be remembered against him; because of the righteousness which he has done, he shall live" (*WEB*, Ezekiel 18:21-22).

We're all guilty of being "wicked" and bad at some point in our lives, and we need to take what we did seriously, then turn ourselves around and walk down the road and actually do what the signs say; stop when it says stop. God said to keep His statutes—which means to live by the Ten Commandments and honor your parents, honor God, honor your neighbor, not lie or steal. We honor God by not gambling away money that's meant to help pay the bills at home and instead honor our family and neighbors with our time and our help.

When the temptation comes to speak badly of others or use foul language, you can stop yourself. You can respect God's commands that give you the power to put your shoulders back and feel the ultimate confidence that by you doing right, you've got the power of God supporting you. When you follow the road signs, follow God's commands to do what's right and good, you reap the rewards of blessings. You don't have to feel guilty, stressed out and worried. You're on the right side and God's got your back. A lost sheep among the hundred is as important as the rest until he returns.

Commitment is the beginning of trusting God. "Commit everything you do to the Lord. Trust Him to help you do it, and He will" (*TLB*, Psalm 37:5). This is about giving thanks, actually giving thanks to God every day without fail because you are grateful deep inside for all that you have. There is not a moment in the day where you aren't feeling grateful and thanking your Greatest Teammate who's pointed out from the dugout about the possibility of the next play and helping you stay focused when you've been pulled out of the game mentally and can't seem to get your stride back. Whether you've noticed, God is with you at every moment. It's always been about you noticing and allowing Him to work in your favor by being thankful for everything you have right now. Commit today, and every day, to waking up first thing in the morning and say, "Thank you, God, for this fantastic day. I commit my day to you, knowing you've got my back."

There's nothing better than some adversity in your life to poke you in the side and remind you God is there to help if you want to accept His help. Part of starting over is accepting you need to start over, then make a commitment to change. This must first be done in the heart, deep inside where you feel the need for change deeply. It's not easy for everyone to feel deeply, so let me explain what this means and what it looks like.

When you were told in school to care about turning in your homework and doing well on tests, there may have seemed a lack of feeling about it at first. Then, when it mattered, and the test was the next day and you found out, it meant whether you were going to be able to play in next week's game, that's when the feeling of anxiety hit. If your grades were usually good enough, remember back to a stressful time when you didn't know if you were going to make the cut. We've all been there, and it's a lonely feeling and no one can help us, but ourselves.

Now take yourself to a time when you felt success after working hard to achieve your goal. It's a great feeling, and it makes us feel strong, but that feeling wanes as soon as we hit another wall and we feel alone again, relying on ourselves to get the answers and work hard to motivate ourselves to succeed the best we can with what we've been given. What we're missing is the most important part of life, the most important teammate in the world—God. When you align yourself with God you expect success, and know that when things don't go your way, or the way you planned it, God has your back and is opening another door to something greater.

DON'T LET FAILURE DISCOURAGE YOU.

IT'S NEVER TOO LATE TO START AGAIN.

I'll be the first one to admit that I made a mistake. At this point, I'm happy to know if I've done something wrong, I'm eager to get it right. I wasn't always this way, and I was caught making excuses, but I knew it was wrong and inevitably the excuses caught up to me like the lies they really are.

Excuses began with the first sin ever committed. *It's in the Bible,* "And He said, 'Have you eaten from the tree that I commanded you not to eat from?' The man said, 'The woman you put here with me—she gave me some fruit from the tree, and I ate it.' Then the Lord God said to the woman, 'What is this you have done?' The woman said, 'The serpent deceived me, and I ate" (*NIV,* Genesis 3:11-13).

Both Adam and Eve were making excuses, passing the buck so to speak to the next person until it landed on the serpent, the greatest liar there ever was. When you pass the blame onto someone else, not accepting you are inevitably part of everything that's happening around you, then you're admitting weakness, admitting to lying and closing the door on growth and success. This is failure.

David L. Angeron

FAILURE IS NOT THE END.

IT'S TIME TO REACH FOR GOD.

If you have failed, no matter how badly, it's not the end and you can reach out and receive immediate help. You have to repose your trust in Jesus.

It's in the Bible, "The steps of good men are directed by the Lord. He delights in each step they take. If they fall it isn't fatal, for the Lord holds them with His hand" (*TLB*, Psalm 37:23-24).

Even good people that try their hardest to be honest, treat others as they'd like to be treated and try to walk with God, sometimes fail. *It's in the Bible*, "The good man does not escape all troubles—he has them too. But the Lord helps him in each and every one" (*TLB*, Psalm 34:19).

You will never be left alone without being shown the best way to solve issues, always given an answer when you wait on God.

Remember, it's not about how many times you fall; it's how many times you get back up. *The Bible assures*. "for though a righteous man falls seven times, he rises again, but the wicked are brought down by calamity" (*NIV*, Proverbs 24:16). Not only is it okay to fall, it's about how you get back up. Are you humbly taking your teammates' hand and shaking off the dust, ready to make the next play? That's how the righteous man falls and gets back up, ready to succeed. Blaming others, cheating on how many reps you do and telling everyone how hard you work is asking for something worse to happen. Take the moment to make the right decision by taking responsibility for all your actions and

The Greatest Teammate

your thoughts, knowing you will succeed next time. "For I can do everything God asks me to with the help of Christ who gives me the strength and power" (*TLB*, Philippians 4:13).

When you decide to start over and make a new way for yourself, that's more honest, more successful and free from the constant strain you're choosing God as your teammate. He will always be there for you, no matter the adversity that is coming against you. With God you are strong and resilient, always able to overcome all the fear and doubt to succeed both in life and in sports. To learn more about how to overcome those roadblocks that come, either in the locker room or at home, keep reading. There's so much more inspiration and stories I want to share with you that will help keep you on the path to success. Start a new story for yourself and have faith in God who is the greatest teammate you'll ever choose.

A clean slate with the eyes of faith
Everybody's got a blank page
A story they're writing today
A wall that they're climbing
You can carry the past on your shoulders
Or you can start over (Flame, 2013).

Chapter 2
ADVERSITY & RESILIENCE

"PRAISE YOU IN THIS STORM,"– CASTING CROWNS

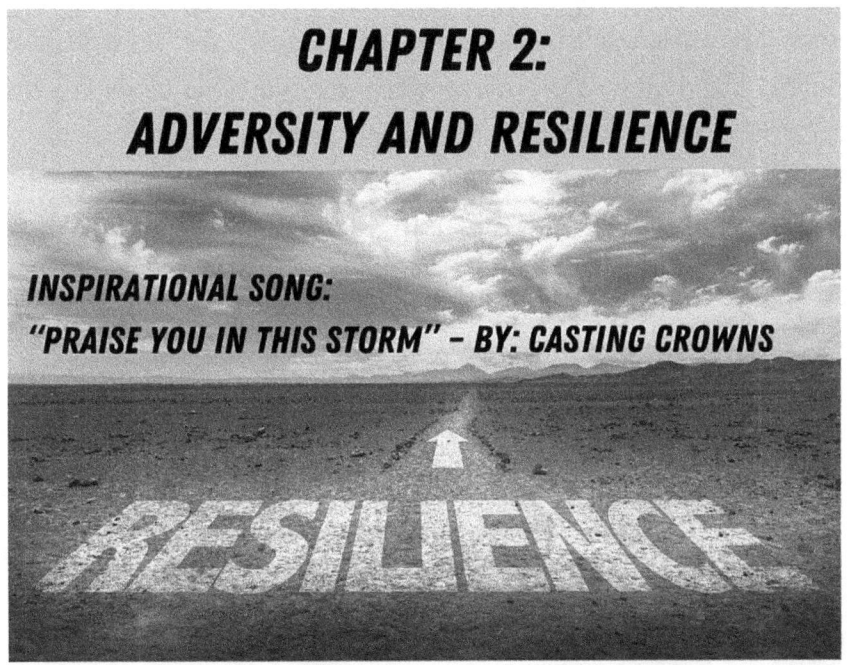

In adversity, we long for prosperity. In prosperity, we fear adversity. Life is the ground where joy and sorrow strive with each other. Meanwhile, our soul perseveres by clinging itself to God. Only he lifts. Only he drowns. Who wishes for troubles? No one. But, it needs to be endured.

St. Augustine asks in Confessions:

Cursed are the prosperities of the world, not once but twice over, because of the fear of adversity and the corruption of success. Cursed are the adversities of the world, not once or twice but thrice, because of the longing for prosperity, because adversity itself is hard, and because of the possibility that one's endurance may crack. Is not human life on earth a trial in which there is no respite? (P. 199)

Adversity is your companion on your path towards success, like the wicked exists alongside the righteous, like the good exists alongside the hostile, like the wheat exists alongside the thistle. One needs to have the discipline. If not, then "you are a poor specimen if you can't stand the pressure of adversity" (*TLB*, Proverb 24:10). You need to be alert. Do not sleep over. Let us keep in mind what has been said in (*TLB*, Proverb 24:30-34):

I walked by the field of a certain lazy fellow and saw that it was overgrown with thorns; it was covered with weeds, and its walls were broken down. Then, as I looked, I learned this lesson:

> *"A little extra sleep,*
> *A little more slumber,*
> *A little folding of the hands to rest."*

means that poverty will break in upon you suddenly like a robber and violently like a bandit.

Now this poverty could be material or spiritual or both. The enemy could be your greed or some money bag who wants to sabotage your game and career. God has commanded you not to waver. Persevere. According to Thomas Aquinas, "To behave with ease in the face of difficult situations is good; but it is also good to endure such situations when they are inevitable" (P.333). The hardship you face can bring pain and sadness, but you have to put up with them instead of letting yourself be bogged down by it. Keep your soul calm in the face of adversity. Don't sap your energy unnecessarily by escaping the situation. Fortitude and patience should be your mantra. It will help you hold firm against fear and grief.

When I was about 9 years old, I had it in my mind that I was going to hit my first home run. I was a skinny, weak kid, but I was fast. I knew it would probably be an inside the park home run, but I swear I could almost taste the spray dirt from the Umpire brushing off the plate after I slid into home. It was so real in my mind and I wanted that home run really bad. Yet, every time I came up to bat something went wrong; the pitcher was no good, my teammates on base in front of me were too slow, and finally, it was the last game of the season. We warmed up on the field and the sun was shining and it was a perfect spring day, but like all weather in the southeast, it turned quickly and it began to rain a little. I was up to bat and instead of the big hit I wanted; I was walked to first. I kept watching the sky and there was talk of a storm, but I finally got back up to bat in the 5th inning and I could still taste it, but this time it'd be a little mud in my mouth instead. I readied myself and walked up to the plate while tilting my head down to keep the rain out, but suddenly lightning struck over the nearby trees and the rain began to really pour down. That was that, and I never got my home run that season.

The Greatest Teammate

It wasn't a big deal to the coach or my parents, but it devastated me and I swore I'd never play baseball again because I was so mad and disappointed. I began to think that I must be just that bad of a player and should just give up on my favorite sport to play.

That's when my mom caught me hanging my head and told me about the scripture (*TLB,* Joshua 1:9), "Yes, be bold and strong! Banish fear and doubt! For remember, the Lord your God is with you wherever you go."

I definitely doubted I was ever going to be good enough to get that home run. And when I returned the next year as a much bigger 10-year-old, I still had a fear of failure. I remembered what my mom said and thought about being patient and strong and how that would get rid of the feelings of fear and doubt. Fortitude is a virtue. It's immediately needed when you have to mediate between the trials of life. It worked, and by our third game, I hit one of many home runs in my career. Sure, I might have still had home runs, but I could have easily given up my favorite sport or never overcome my doubt. Adversity has come and gone many times in my life, but having the knowledge in my heart and mind that God is there with me wherever I go has kept me from falling down and staying down; I always get back up knowing I have the God-given power to accomplish my goals. You need strength of mind when your human will is shaken. As Seneca writes in his letters, "We do not fail to dare because they're difficult; they're difficult because we do not dare" (P. 225).

As for your mind, your soul needs to be strengthened. Let me remind you, it's not a hope based on false premises. It's the hope that comes from the given skills you have, like a soldier who has the skill and training to come out of a hostile situation. You acquire skills through relentless practice. Fear would naturally vanish when you think you're confident against any adverse situation. Now there's another kind of bravery, which you show impulsively, which is an act out of anger, out of passion in the face of loss. There's one more where you have chosen your spirit to be resilient out of choice, out of your devotion towards your work with God by your side. Here your soul strengthens against any infirmities. Faith can move mountains. Have no doubt.

Adversity comes in many forms and most aren't crushed dreams of a 9-year-old. They're crushed dreams of that can subvert your career, end relationships, and leave you without the means to pay your rent. Will you give in when someone says you're done, just because they think you're done? It takes resilience, sometimes an amazing amount of resilience, to stand up against adversity and prove it wrong, prove that you're stronger and better. And with God at your side, with your heart filled with gratitude and humility, you can overcome any obstacle.

Most people don't realize that they need Jesus until they hit rock bottom or face adversity that life will throw at them. God doesn't give you problems that you cannot handle. He made us strong, and most problems or storms are valuable lessons that we need to learn from.

I was sure by now, God, you would have reached down
And wiped our tears away,
Stepped in and saved the day.
But once again, I say amen
That it's still raining
As the thunder rolls
I barely hear your whisper through the rain
I'm with you (Casting Crowns, 2005)

When I mention Jesus, it means God's son who was sent here to earth to show us how humans were doing it all wrong, worshipping material idols and living sinful lives that led to chaos, confusion, and living falsely.

When we doubt our faith and our abilities, we consistently worry over what's coming, and what obviously hasn't happened yet. It's called a game of what-if-ing and it's a test of your faith. It's easy to worry and think, "What if I can't pull this off" or "What if I screw it up"? You can play this game all day long, wasting time and energy simply worrying about something you can't control.

There's no need to worry—God has everything under control

Truth is a means of purification. It's the light of the sun. Its value comes from the good, as Simone Wile speaks in her book Lectures on Philosophy (P. 195). The truth is with God everything is possible (*TLB*, Mark 10:27) It's in the Bible, "So don't worry at all about having enough food and clothing. Why be like the heathen? For they take pride in all these things and are deeply concerned about them. But your heavenly Father already knows perfectly well that you need them, and He will give them to you if you give Him first place in your life and live as He wants you to" *(TLB,* Matthew 6:31-33).

LET GO AND LET GOD

At first glance, this might seem like you can go ahead and park yourself on the couch and let God do the work, but it's the opposite. It's like saying the glass is half empty, seeing the lack of water. Instead, the phrase "let go and let God" is about seeing the glass half full and ready for you to drink. You need to think rightly about it, know there's always abundance in what God gives us, and reach out to take the glass.

We should "seek first the kingdom of God and his righteousness, and all these things will be added to you" (*CSB*, Mathew 6:33). There's no need to obsess over our needs, as God will take care of them. On the other hand, we do have the responsibility to work toward meeting our needs. We are asked to exercise the abilities God has given to us. And it's important to realize that He is meeting our needs, not ourselves.

The Greatest Teammate

When we cling to our adversities, our problems that keep us from living a successful life, we are making the problem more important than God; more important than our own growth and movement forward to something better.

Wrapping yourself up in a constant battle with your inability to get along with a new coach or teammate that's hindering your best performance is only going to bury you further. We all experience someone walking into our lives and making it miserable. What do we do about it? Get in their face when they do something we think is wrong or just talk about them behind their back? This is when it's time to let go and let God.

Let go of the anger, the disappointment, the frustration, and your inability to solve the problem that faces you. It's a good time to pray and ask God for direction.

David L. Angeron

It's always a good time to stop and pray!

And while you're waiting in God's direction, praying daily and keeping your thought close to God's, let go of your own preconceived worries and judgments to let God do His work, not only within your heart but others. Keep showing up and diligently working and listening, staying focused on your work, and doing your very best. Soon the answer will come. Be ready to follow His direction and be grateful you have the Greatest Teammate on your side, working everything out for the good of everyone. You shouldn't be afraid to take a good part in the hardship you face and see it to a good end. It isn't what you endure that matters, but how you endure it.

I remember when I stumbled in the wind
You heard my cry you raised me up again (Casting Crowns, 2005)

Some adverse situations come into our lives and knock us straight down to the bottom. The failure we see in ourselves is almost too great to take, and there doesn't seem to be a way out, or a way to come clean.

Our problem is final, so it seems. That's what's so beautiful about reaching out of the darkness with humility, up to God, asking for forgiveness and help. Forgiveness for doubting God ever existed, maybe even blaming Him erroneously for what happened.

He created you and knows you best, and has given you the power of resilience in times of trouble. You simply need to reach out with your heart and mind and ask Him for help. When you stumble in the wind of life that knocks you down, He will hear your cry and raise you up again. You'll find you're stronger than you thought, and there is an answer to your problems.

Waiting on God to do His work and resolve issues that we're facing while we continue to do our work can take patience. We fall back into worrying, feeling anxiety over our issues, and doubt all over again. Worry doesn't accomplish anything. *It's in the Bible,* "Stop your anger! Turn off your wrath. Don't fret and worry—it only leads to harm" (*TLB,* Psalm 37:8). You must have the consolation for enduring what is right, and you will not dwell on its suffering that it causes. If someone asks you, why do you have to persevere? You tell them you persevere, that you can teach your teammate how to endure. You don't wish to have false belief and seek blessings on behalf of it. You don't have a vacant mind that dreams deceptively of the riches of the world. You see the truth, unadorned, unvarnished, that is not ugly, that will not dazzle you or deceive you. You're not ignorant of the adversities. You know how to face it? You have first ridden yourself of anger, as advised by Jesus. So you don't worry.

Worrying is a waste of time

Think about it: when you're worried, are you actually accomplishing anything? You're misled to believe your what-if-ing game works out solutions, but it's not. Worrying is a waste of time. Some say certain restlessness is natural to men. That's why their mind wanders aimlessly. Don't get caught in the whirlpool of thoughts that lead you nowhere. In fact, adversities test your resolve and help you plant your feet firmly on the ground. *It's in the Bible,* "And besides, what's the use of worrying? What good does it do? Will it add a single day to your life? Of course not! And if worry can't even do such little things as that, what's the use of worrying over bigger things" (*TLB,* Luke 12:25-26)?

David L. Angeron

We cannot remove worry until we replace it with something better—prayer.

Letting go, especially for those of us that like a sense of control this is difficult but with practice and a lot of faith you're opening up the door to let God do His perfect work. Can you remember a time and situation where you tried one idea after the next to solve a problem and it still didn't work out? Maybe by the third try you sort of got somewhere? What if I told you that instead of over thinking and trying out every solution that popped into your head randomly, you spent that time getting other, more productive work done, and let your mind rest in thoughts of gratitude for all the good already in your life? You can relax, feel joy, and keep being productive while listening for God's direction on how best to solve the issues.

Many times in my life I've experienced amazing healing after much prayer where instead of me having to lift a finger to solve a problem, it solved itself! This is what happens when you let go, keep praying and working, and let God take care of it.

One season I had a player that came to practices with a grumpy attitude and acted like he was too good to be there. Soon as game day came, he was 100% better and played amazing. Thing is, those practices were important, and he was ruining them with his bad attitude and laziness. My initial reaction was to list ways I could help change him, like running him until he was too tired to be bad-tempered, but experience with God always having the best solution led me to pray instead.

There were many times when I had to put my own annoyance in check and see him as God's own creation, too. After a couple of weeks, we had a game against our biggest competitor and he choked at bat and dropped the ball twice. Instead of his usual ego trip attitude, he was visibly crumbling and looked like he was about to give up entirely. Several of his teammates started encouraging him, in the dugout they gathered around him in support. Suddenly, he was grinning and I could see that it was the genuine care and encouragement from his teammates that was healing him. I could never have given him that, or forced the players to do something so genuine. Only God can do the real healing.

We're just here to let God work through us to heal others.

The only way this healing takes place through us is if we stop worrying and pray. *It's in the Bible,* "Don't worry about anything; instead pray about everything; tell God your needs and don't forget to thank Him for His answers. If you do this, you will experience God's peace, which is far more wonderful than the human mind can understand. His peace will keep your thoughts and your hearts quiet and at rest as you trust in Christ Jesus" (*TLB,* Philippians 4:6-7).

When you pray, give all your worries to the Lord.

"Let Him have all your worries and cares, for He is always thinking about you and watching everything that concerns you"
(TLB, 1 Peter 5:7).

What worry do you have right now that you'd like to be free of and that God can take away for you? Take the time right now to write down your worries and the issues that are bothering you.

Next, write down what you'll do to keep striving toward successfully overcoming the problems? For example, pray morning and night and whenever the thoughts of worry come into my head. Keep working hard and be a good person.

There's a lot of temptation in the world, and there's the easy way and the hard way. Being the underdog, the one down and out and not expected to win is a tough place to rise from, and the temptation to do it the easy way is very high. Do you have what it takes to take the difficult road where you have to trust in God and be patient? Let's explore how you can go from underdog to winner in the next chapter. Don't wait until tomorrow; let's do this today!

The Greatest Teammate

Chapter 3
UNDERDOG

Underdog—
by Audio Adrenaline

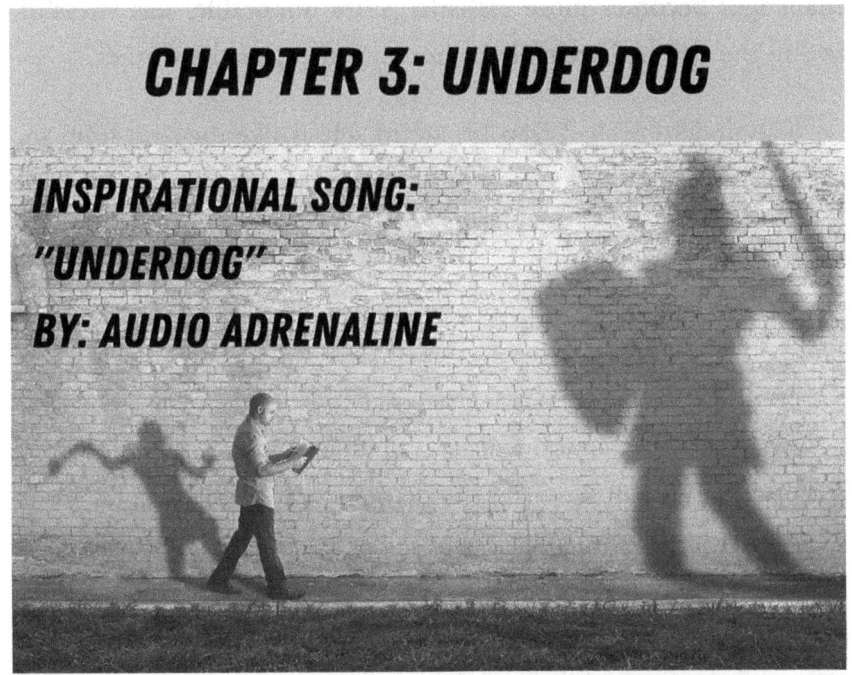

Every time we turn on the TV, radio, search the Web, or hang out on social media, there is temptation everywhere, seemingly there to distract us from our path. Being an underdog is always tough, in sports and in life. Being the underdog can do two things: push you to give up and submit to the temptation, or make you work harder to overcome the challenge. An underdog is not a deceiver. He is not too proud to become blind to his own blindness. He is not deluded into self-designation, or conceited. He knows with you Lord 'is the wisdom' (*TLB,* Job 12:13). He persists. He works on his errors and doesn't hide it under colorful names. His small successes are humbling. He understands that he's not just the physical embodiment of a creature. He is also a spiritual creature.

He understands that with God as his teammate, overcoming the challenges becomes more realistic, more honorable, less stressful, and in the end he inevitably comes out on top as the winner.

The underdog shall reap his award. He is like the seed from the Parable of Seed and Harvest from (Mark 4:26-29), that through the grace of God it keeps working on itself hidden from the eyes of the world, and one day sprouts into a glorious harvest that the world reaps its award. Everyone rejoices.

An underdog is a person or group that is expected to lose. The team or individual expected to win is the top dog. And when the underdog wins, we call this an upset. The underdog unexpectedly comes out on top and surprises everyone. Some call it the Rocky moment, made famous by the movie franchise Rocky. It's a modern take on the Bible story of David and Goliath where David was the underdog; a small, young boy brave and filled with faith in God's power to overcome any obstacle pitted himself against the giant wreaking havoc on his people named Goliath. I recommend reading the story again in the Bible (1 Samuel: 17). It's different from days in Sunday school when you're young, and only the actual battle seemed interesting. Scripture we think we know and don't have to read again can actually spur you to positive action, change your life in an instant as a surge of God's loving reassurance can touch us and you see the story come to life within you.

David and Goliath is a very heroic story that inspires us all to hold fast to our faith, keep being and doing well, and listen for God's directions on how to overcome the Goliath in our lives. It's a powerful and true metaphor that with one simple river stone launched from a slingshot in a moment where David overcame all fear and could upset the enemy. This is you. You also have that close relationship with God, all the faith to move mountains and bravely face your enemy as you listen, then take action in God's direction for you.

We all can do the same. We're *expected* to do the very same as David and put ourselves and our egos aside, stand up to the temptation that there is something greater or better than God, and stamp it out.

Jesus told us "ye shall do greater" (*KJV,* John 14:12), and that is what we are tasked to do, but we can't do it alone on only our human will and human ideas we think are so brilliant. We must pray, have faith, listen, then take action on God's direction for us every day.

Sure, we all deserve a break and time to kick back and enjoy life after working so hard and doing everything we can to be a great person—a great teammate. The world, filled with its temptations to cheat, take the simple way, lie or waste our time gambling when there's a family at home waiting for us, this is the Goliath in our times. It wreaks havoc on our communities and our families, breaking them apart and making us weaker.

The Greatest Teammate

It might not seem fair being the underdog, but it's our job to be humble and fight the good fight against Goliath every day. **Life is not always fair.** *It's in the Bible*, "Again I looked throughout the earth and saw that the swiftest person does not always win the race, nor the strongest man in battle, and that wise men are often poor, and skillful men are not necessarily famous" (*TLB*, Ecclesiastes 9:11)

Whenever I hear of an Underdog Story, I'm always reminded of the story of Joseph in the Bible who was the underdog in his family. Eventually, he was thrown into a pit and sold into slavery by his brothers. In a foreign land, now in slavery and told what to do and made to work for his owner every day, Joseph seemed to have no chance of getting home, let alone live a life of his own. Though the odds were against him, he was still in the game and ready to win. I'll be referring to this story of Joseph several times in this book because each part of Joseph's story has important connections to your life today and how this book can help lead you to victory over every obstacle thrown at you.

In order to get the most out of reading this book and stepping up in life, it's imperative that you set goals for yourself. Goals are not a long list of stuff you need to accomplish; it's a living testament and commitment that is both material and incorporeal (that which cannot be touched, like your feelings and spirit). It is incredibly powerful to create goals and connect with them on a deeper level.

YOU MUST EMOTIONALLY CONNECT TO YOUR GOALS & DESIRES. SUCCESS IS 100% LINKED TO YOUR FEELINGS

The key to your success that I'll repeat several times as well is that you need to create an emotional connection before you can see results. You need to FEEL that desire to win, the desire to be better, the desire to have some happiness, and be free of anxiety.

Thing is, you were probably told when you were young that emotions didn't belong on the field, or in the classroom, or even at home. Emotions can "make you sloppy and unfocused", adults will tell you after you've missed a catch, got in trouble at school or got angry at home and yelled at your parents. It's not about NOT having emotions, it's about controlling your emotions. Emotions signal stress and are simply information for you so that you can deal with what's coming at you. Without emotions, you're a robot, and though that might seem like a safe thing to be so you're not getting in trouble and seem focused on the ball, it's often a sign that you're not invested enough, not willing to push yourself harder and farther. You need emotions for that; controlled emotions.

HOW TO CONTROL EMOTIONS

ANGER

This is the big one—anger. At first, it can feel really good to be angry and let it out. The voice in your head probably told you, "you have every right to be angry!" Justifications like these are endless and they don't offer any real solution to the problem, just you looking like a fool that can't control himself.

HOW ARE YOU EMOTIONALLY?

You come home from an exhausting day and all you want to do is sit down on the couch with a snack; you're starving. When you walk in the door, you notice your roommate and their friends have trashed the place and you don't have a place to sit on the couch (there's your bag of chips emptied all over the seat.) Your roommate walks in and you.

1) You lay into him right away, asking him what the heck he was thinking, that's your stuff. He shrugs his shoulders and says he'll clean it up later as he heads out the door. You're beyond mad.

a) *EMOTIONALLY HOT*

2) Feel like smacking him, but tell yourself he's a good guy and calm down. You ask him to clean the place up and replace your chips. He says he has to leave and will do it later, which basically means you'll be cleaning up the mess, so you lay into him about being a slob and threaten him about replacing the chips.

a) ENABLER

3) Are totally unhappy with the situation, but you've made messes too so after you ask him to clean it up and replace your chips and he says he's got to take off for the night you begrudgingly clean up his mess and figure you'll get yours by having some of his food and won't clean the bathroom when it's your turn.

a) PASSIVE AGGRESSIVE

4) You say nothing and do nothing with the mess; you leave it for him to clean it. You have a stash of extra chips in your bedroom and that's where you go to relax so none of it bothers you.

a) ROBOT

Each of these types of emotional responses is legitimate, and it's just your natural tendency to react one way or another. Recognizing these in yourself, being able to honestly point it out when you submit to these emotions in the very moment they come up and instead of letting them overcome you, you overcome them. You're the master of your emotions, and God has commanded you to do so. The Bible says, "Brothers, I do not consider that I have made it my own. But one thing I do: forgetting what lies behind and straining forward to what lies ahead, I press on toward the goal for the prize of the upward call of God in Christ Jesus. Let those of us who are mature think this way, and if in anything you think otherwise, God will reveal that also to you" (*ESV,* Philippians 3:13-15). You silently strive towards your goal even when you're beaten up and down. When this song by Audio Adrenaline aptly defines you:

The Greatest Teammate

Been beat up
Been broken down
Nowhere but up
When you're face down
On the ground
I'm in last place
If I place at all
But there's hope for this underdog!
That's the way, uh-huh, we like it!
That's the way, uh-huh, we like it!
You can call me the underdog (1999).

Then you must remember Josh Hamilton. He was drafted right out of high school with the first overall pick by the Tampa Bay Devil Rays in the 1999 Major League Baseball Draft, and everyone had huge expectation from him. But he couldn't control what was about to come.

Hamilton was injured in a car accident before the 2001 season, and the pernicious injury bogged him down for the next two years. That was only the beginning. He became addicted to cocaine in 2003 and was off the field repeatedly for violating the MLB drug policy. It was hard for him to kick his habit, and he could play baseball for another three years until 2006.

But God has some plan made for him. It was an emotional confrontation with his grandmother which brought him to senses. Hamilton got his act together and was traded to the Cincinnati Reds in 2006. In 2007, eight years after being drafted, he finally made his major league debut. The Reds traded him to the Texas Rangers in 2008, and since then, Hamilton has established himself as one of the top outfielders in baseball. He won the AL MVP Award in 2010 after hitting .359 with 32 home runs and 100 RBI as he helped lead his team to its first World Series. It's hard to not root for this underdog story. Was it just out of luck that he had achieved his entire feat? No, he must have set some goal for himself. If you want to believe the words of Derek Jeter:

I love digging my spikes into the brown clay; I love how the light frames the field, and I even love the smell of hot dogs and hot pretzels that wafts down on us. Then there are the creative fans, who are the loudest I've ever heard and who make us feel special during every game. . . . Most of my life was spent working toward that elusive goal of becoming a major leaguer, and most of my life now is spent on keeping me here at a high level. My goal is simple: to keep getting better. . . . I like to chase my dreams, and I advise everyone else to do the same. It all starts with setting goals—we all need them. Whether your goal is to play for the Yankees or to win the pie-eating contest at summer camp, goals motivate us to do better. My ultimate dream was to play major-league baseball, but I had smaller goals along the way.

Jeter advises his followers and those who want to become a baseball player that all good accomplishments start with goals. He tells his readers to ask themselves some very important questions just as early as they can: What do they love to do? What are they especially good at? Setting goals that are both dreams and future realities is one of the hardest tasks in life.

The goals are not going to be easy. Pain and failure are part of the game. The world is also not fair. They move as the stars of your success move. If failure scares you; you will remain scared forever. So I advise you to develop the habit of listening, thinking, and learning.

You must be serious about your game. Have fun too. You must be a leader, but you also develop the habit to follow. Above all, aim at righteousness, godliness, faith, love, steadfastness, gentleness (*RSV,* 1Timothy 6:11).

SETTING GOALS

It's the process of accomplishing goals through a defined aim and action. Then comes the refinement of the goal and moving further through honest evaluation. The objective is to enhance the performance towards a larger goal on an unconscious level. Having a realistic goal also works as a motivating factor. It also keeps the athlete stress free by giving the athlete a purpose and direction. The benefit of goal setting is that the progress can also be measured. If you're playing a team game, like baseball, then by keeping up with your performance you can also bring positivity to the team.

If we have to define what a goal is then, "goals are like magnets that attract us to higher ground and new horizons. They give our eyes a focus, our mind an aim, and our strength a purpose. Without their pull, we would remain forever stationary, incapable of moving forward. A goal is a possibility that fulfills a dream" (Kennedy 1998; Burton & Raedeke, p.52).

According to Sports Psychology, there are three broad goal types: outcome goals, performance goals, and process goals.

Outcome goals are about outperforming other competitors. The objective of winning represents the predominant outcome goal; reaching a final, or simply beating a teammate in an individual game, also represents examples of outcome goals.

Performance goals are based on personal achievement and are entirely subjective. Typical performance goals are to run a race at a certain time, to jump a certain distance, to lift a specific weight, or to do a number of repetitions in a training situation.

Process goals are also subjective. Its main focus is on the process of performing better rather than achieving a predetermined goal. For example, they might range from the breathing techniques designed to master mental side of the game, to imaging in the mind's eye of getting a home run in the next game.

Outcome goal is the destination, like a beacon of light. Performance and process goals are the process to achieve the outcome goal. Disaster follows if the focus is only on the outcome goal. Why? Because, you have partial control over the outcome. I am calling it partial because you have worked diligently towards it. In a way, you have been involved. So what's important here? The important factor is focusing on the process and performance of the game.

Benefits of Goal Setting:

» Goals enhance focus and concentration.
» Goals boost self-confidence.
» Goals help prevent or manage stress.
» Goals help create a positive mental attitude.
» Goals increase intrinsic motivation to excel.
» Goals improve the quality of practices by making training more challenging.
» Goals enhance playing skill, techniques, and strategies.
» Goals improve overall performance.

Control and Flexibility

An athlete should control the kind of goal he or she is setting for themselves—the goal he could achieve in the given time—so that they can take credit for their success. There are so many variables working here to keep in mind. The performance of the athlete who has won the game for his team is important, so does the performance of other teammates. Owner, coach, and referee are also important. Luck also plays its part. God has his own plan for you. So having a goal that you can personally control yourself is important. For example, it's in your control if you have to practice six days a week. There's every bit possibility of getting an injury while training. Hence, process is important. The goal should also be flexible so that you can raise it or reduce it while evaluating your performance. You will get more motivation if the goal you have set for yourself is more challenging.

Measurable Goals

In order to have a controllable and flexible goal, you must set yourself a measurable goal. If a pitcher has set an average speed of 80 mph in his training, then he has to keep at it consistently. The best trick to measure your performance is by avoiding do-your-best yardstick. Don't go home with a motivation that you did your best. It will make you consistent with your performance and help you not to fall into a deluded trap. You need to keep a few things in mind: keep in check the quality and quantity of your performance, observe your performance objectively and subjectively too, also keep a check on your behavior with your teammate and how you have evolved as a person.

Guidelines for Setting Effective Goals

- » Give higher priority to process and performance goals as a higher goal than outcome goals.
- » Set specific, measurable goals rather than general or "do-your-best" goals.
- » Set moderately difficult goals that are challenging but realistic.
- » Set positive goals.

» Set both long-term and short-term goals. Short-term goals will serve as the building blocks for reaching long-term goals.
» Set both individual and team goals, with individual goals take role-specific steps to attain team goals.
» Set both practice and competitive goals, with practice goals focusing on developing skills and competitive goals geared to performing better.

Goal setting is not achieve them-forget them. It's more than that. It requires comprehensive implementation. You have got talent, implement it judiciously, practice and hone your skills, make yourself better. Don't sit idle and gloat over your talent that having a mere talent would take you across over the success side.

The gift of talent, which you have been given, has to be used for a good purpose. You have to realize your 'self' and strive for excellence. As it has been said in The bible, "Finally, brothers, whatever is true, whatever is honorable, whatever is just, whatever is pure, whatever is lovely, whatever is commendable, if there is any excellence, if there is anything worthy of praise, think about these things" (*ESV,* Philippians 4:8). Have no doubt about what has been said in The Bible. Jesus shows his affinity towards the underdogs, "⁷ some rich people are poor, and some poor people have great wealth" (*TLB,* Proverb 13:7)!

David L. Angeron

I'm in this race to win a prize
The odds against me
The world has plans for my demise
What they don't see is
That a winner is not judged
By his small size
But by the
Substitute he picks to
Run the race
And mine's already won
Underdog, I wince every time I say the word
Especially in connection with Jesus
Yet, as I read the birth stories about Jesus
(I've got freedom, I've got freedom)
I cannot help but conclude that although the world may be tilted towards the rich and the powerful
God, hallelujah, in the prophecy
Is still the Lord behind us all (Audio Adrenaline, 1999)!

The Greatest Teammate

Chapter 4

Faced with Doubt

"Voice of Truth" – by Casting Crowns

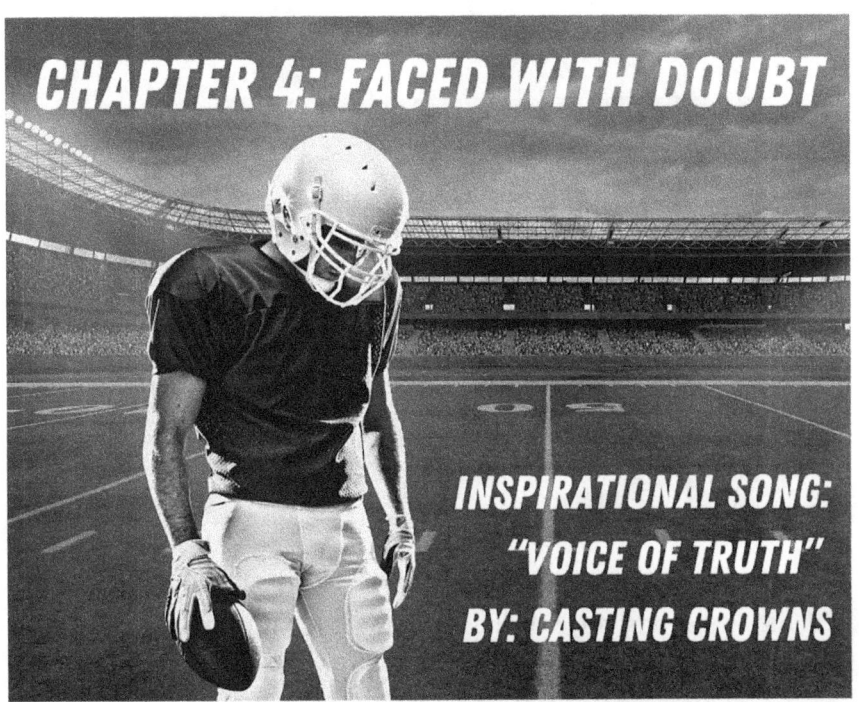

We are living in a world filled with negativity, doubting ourselves and others. We can doubt our own motives, and our own competence. Doubts can have serious implications on our self-confidence. The first thing we know about ourselves is our imperfections. It's not possible to isolate our thoughts and judge them. So, it's not impossible to judge erroneously. That is where negative thoughts creep in, because we're assessing ourselves based on our own judgment. Since we're a rational being, we think, "How can our judgment be impaired"? When we realize it was, our confidence becomes low. Suddenly, we subject ourselves to incoherent and conflicting thoughts. The living world appears as an obstacle to our mind.

Then it becomes hard to hear God's voice over the noise. You can't hear the wondrous voice of the one who hears the cries of the world. The voice that surpasses all the voices of the world, you pray your mind to be attuned to that voice. You wish to put aside all doubts and meditate on the pure and the holy, because he's your only reliance in the time of pain and sufferings.

Thomas Aquinas elucidates his point on faith and on those who doubt:

In fact, faith must often take the place of knowledge in our assertions. Not only may certain truths be believed by the ignorant and known by scholars, but it also happens, because of the weakness of our understanding and the wanderings of our imagination, error creeps into our inquiry. Many a person misconceives conclusions of a proof, and so remains in doubt about truths that are in fact well demonstrated. For such a person, the fact that reputedly wise persons disagree over the same questions is completely baffling. So it was good that providence should lay down as truths of faith a number of truths accessible to reason, so that everyone might easily share in the knowledge of God without fear of doubt or error (P. 18).

When you are attempting to redirect your life to develop a relationship with God, you will have people telling you that you can't win. People will doubt your ideas and motives at every attempt to walk in faith with God. The torment you suffer affects your body and mind. The doubt cripples our mind that whether we would be able to find satisfaction in our lives or not. We think the worst of the situation. The only expedient cure is that we need to interpret the best of whatever is doubtful in that situation.

Just like in sports, you should not worry about what others think of you, and you shouldn't seek approval from anyone that you wouldn't ask for advice. In the game of life, the only voice that matters is the one from above — God's voice. Trust in the Lord with all your heart and do not lean on your own understanding. In all your ways acknowledge him, and he will make your paths straight. Be not wise in your own eyes; fear the Lord and turn away from evil. It will be healing to your flesh and refreshment to your bones (*ESV,* Proverb 3:5-8).

The most beautiful of passage of the Gospel that you could get across is from (*ESV,* Matthew 25:31-40):

[31] "When the Son of Man comes in his glory, and all the angels with him, then he will sit on his glorious throne. [32] Before him will be gathered all the nations, and he will separate people one from another as a shepherd separates the sheep from the goats. [33] And he will place the sheep on his right, but the goats on the left. [34] Then the King will say to those on his right, 'Come, you who are blessed by my Father, inherit the kingdom prepared for you from the foundation of the world. [35] For I was hungry, and you gave me food, I was thirsty and you gave me drink, I was a stranger and you welcomed me, [36] I was naked and you clothed me, I was sick and you visited me, I was in prison and you came to me.' [37] Then the righteous will answer him, saying, 'Lord, when did we see you hungry and feed you, or thirsty and give you drink? [38] And when did we see you a stranger and welcome you, or naked and clothe you? [39] And when did we see you sick or in prison and visit you?' [40] And the King will answer them, 'Truly, I say to you, as you did it to one of the least of these my brothers, you did it to me.'

The Parable asks of you not to doubt your 'self' when people judge you and be on the righteous path. Leave your doubt to him as you will be with him on the right on the Judgment Day. You want to cast your doubt away: Love your neighbor and understand the pain and suffering of the people around you. The neighbor is your teammate. The neighbor is anyone who needs help at hand.

David L. Angeron

I encourage you to listen closely to the song "Voice of Truth" by Casting Crowns and pick out the meaning as it relates to you.

> *To climb out of this boat I'm in*
> *Onto the crashing waves*
> *To step out of my comfort zone*
> *Into the realm of the unknown where Jesus is*
> *And He's holding out His hand*
> *But the waves are calling out my name*
> *And they laugh at me*
> *Reminding me of all the times*
> *I've tried before and failed*
> *The waves they keep on telling me*
> *Time and time again. "Boy, you'll never win!"*
> *"You'll never win!" (2003)*

The lyrics mention the waves as a metaphor for people in your life that can often become the negative voice in our head that has an opinion and negative criticism about what you're attempting to do. Have you ever stopped and took a moment to recognize this voice that only you can hear inside your head that mimics what you've heard from people?

Let's break this insidious voice down to its roots so you can uproot it and toss it in the trash where it belongs. Basically, it's the devil on your shoulder that continues to whisper in your ear, suggesting stupid, bad, negative, get-yourself-in-trouble ideas. It's your job to constantly, and I mean minute-to-minute, cast these thoughts out because they are not God's thoughts and they are not your thoughts. They don't belong to you, and they are not you.

The same goes for people shaming, belittling, or criticizing your sincere methods and path toward greatness. You will fail to deliver sometimes, even with the best intentions, and the only way out of temporary setbacks is to cast away the doubt that wants to immediately creep in and say, "See, you can't do this. I knew it all along." And it doesn't help when someone in the crowd tells you, "You should quit. Give it up."

The first thing you do is control your thoughts. For example, you can say aloud to the person and to yourself, "I don't quit." You also doubt the capacity of other's judgment of you. No one is so farsighted. Only God is. "Jesus immediately reached out his hand and took hold of him, saying to him, "O you of little faith, why did you doubt" (*ESV*, Matthew 14:31)? Even if you have the faith of a mustard seed, you will find shade under its tree when it grows. Your relationship with God will be restored. You must learn that you're not an expert, and you're ready to revise your previous doubting self for better. Only then you would be able to find coherence in your thought. Only then your belief in yourself and God would become firm. If there's a paradox in your thought, like I can see a cat at a distance; I am not farsighted—it's pretty evident that you can't judge the unreliability of your thought; hence the improvement of your self-belief will be difficult. So make learning and unlearning a lifelong process.

You have to keep this up because the devil will want to whisper in your ear again tomorrow. And insecure people that don't know any better will say ignorant and mean things the next game. It's entirely up to you to deny the negatives suggestions, replace them with positive replies, and recognize God's all-powerful omnipresence in your life and everyone's lives. Then keep moving toward your goals. Learn from the life of Jesus—when John the Baptist was in the prison and had doubts about Jesus as described in (*ESV,* Luke 7: 19-23) "And John, [19] calling two of his disciples to him, sent them to the Lord, saying, "Are you the one who is to come, or shall we look for another?" [20] And when the men had come to him, they said, "John the Baptist has sent us to you, saying, 'Are you the one who is to come, or shall we look for another?'" [21] In that hour he healed many people of diseases and plagues and evil spirits, and on many who were blind he bestowed sight. [22] And he answered them, "Go and tell John what you have seen and heard: the blind received their sight, the lame walk, lepers are cleansed, and the deaf hear, the dead are raised up, the poor have good news preached to them. [23] And blessed is the one who is not offended by me." What did you see, when a doubt was cast?

Jesus went on to cure a blind and bestowed sight to the blind. He cleared the doubt of John the Baptist through his miraculous deed.

A coaching friend of mine shared a story of a player that had a brother that was always teasing him and picking at everything he did. It was sort of a family thing to tease and even wrestle it out if an argument couldn't be solved. Generally, it was fine, and the player felt he had a good family, but the negative talk, the teasing, started to get into his own head. One Sunday family dinner he walked in through the front door and instantly his brother was making fun of his lame outfit and he replied, "I can't say much for yours either." Then his brother mentioned how he was a better player than he was. "You know

The Greatest Teammate

how you are at the end of a game when it's tight. You always choke. I'm popping off home runs. You suck so much more than me."

This player then came up in the bottom of the 9th, game tied, and you know what thought ran through his head while he stared down the pitcher? "You always choke. You know how you are when the game is tight." It sounded just like his brother, but this time it came across as his own voice. An accusatory voice that was there to make him doubt his ability to perform to his best ability, and a voice that was trying to make him doubt that his Greatest Teammate was not there to support him in every moment. How can you arrive at a satisfactory conclusion when the words used against you are indifferent and lame? How can you maintain the decorum of language and keep it sublime? Don't let the enemy with its lying words get in between you and God. Don't rest on the kind of aspersion, which has been cast upon you. It may appeal to your laziness when you imbibe the pernicious thought of others and make it yours.

It can have severe consequences on you if you don't act. Melancholy, sadness, and depression would be the consequences of the gloomy view. Or you labor hard and surmount all evil thoughts. Use your mental power, bring your passion to your help, and charge your soul with the words of good Lord. There is a famous line written by Sartre in his play No exit, "Hell is other people" (P.45). He is not saying the people are hell, but the opinion and judgment in which they trap you is hell. You start seeing yourselves from their eyes, the kind of vision they have for you. The only remedy is to follow your passion, let's say baseball, with all the passion and the purity of your heart. What do I mean by the purity of the heart? I mean to say follow your game without thinking of any profits attached to it: fame, glory, and money, whatever it is.

It's the same as if you're pursuing your love and friendship. Does anyone fall in love for profit, or for the sake of ambition and glory? It's desirable on its own account.

If you love your game, please don't lower its dignity. Respect the game and follow it with a pure heart. The same way you love God. You don't need any kind of wisdom to love. Even if you lack any, the Lord says in (*ESV*, James 1:5-8), "If any of you lacks wisdom, let him ask God, who gives generously to all without reproach, and it will be given him. But let him ask in faith, with no doubt, for the one who doubts is like a wave of the sea that is driven and tossed by the wind. For that person must not suppose that he will receive anything from the Lord; he is a double-minded man, unstable in all his ways."

A Sunday school teacher once told me that because we are made in God's likeness we are powerful, divine in reflection, and "wonderfully made." The Sunday school teacher also said that when we doubt ourselves or someone causes us to doubt our abilities, we doubt God. God created you. If you doubt yourself, you're not open to receive God's blessings because you cut him off. Push the doubt away, pull the truth in.

It can take courage to stand up to the voices of the crowd, that one person who you thought cared about you, or the voice in your head making you crazy. All the emotional dissonance comes from your mind. It is needlessly troubled by what awaits. Your thoughts race ahead while you cope with the present. Whatever good that is left in you, turns into darkness. You're not an animal who sees a danger and runs away. The danger vanishes for an animal when it's not around. But for humans, the future and past both haunt in equal measures. At this point in time, being able to stand up for truth, for God, and tell them all "NO!" can take guts. Courage must be grounded in the strength of the Lord. *It's in the Bible*, (*NKJV*, Deuteronomy 31:6), "Be strong and of good courage, do not fear nor be afraid of them; for the Lord your God, He is the One who goes with you. He will not leave you nor forsake you." He will not abandon you, leave you to suffer without reaching out to help you rise and conquer the doubt because you are His creation and He loves you.

> *But the voice of truth tells me a different story*
> *The voice of truth says, "Do not be afraid!"*
> *The voice of truth says, "This is for My glory"*
> *Out of all the voices calling out to me*
> *I will choose to listen and believe the voice of truth*
> *(Casting Crowns, 2003).*

My primary goal is to help athletes build life skills through sports. There isn't sport without life skills in place first. When it's appropriate, I add lessons for building an athlete's relationship with God, as this is the base from which to build your life skills up, and then build your career, enjoying success on and off the field. Sport doesn't come first. Your girlfriend doesn't come first. Sport can't dictate how to live life. Your family and loved ones certainly can't dictate your life, nor save you from what life can throw at you. With God everything is possible, as it is said in (*ESV*, Matthew 19:26):

[26] But Jesus looked at them and said, "With man this is impossible, but with God all things are possible."

Only a solid relationship with God can root you so deeply that nothing in this world can move you. Courage and confidence are born of daily connection with God and living out the truths set out in the Bible. "For the Lord will be your confidence and will keep your foot from being caught" (*ESV*, Proverb 3:26).

The Greatest Teammate

A really important exercise that I teach in my Mental Master Training is to work with eliminating doubt and replacing it with true confidence. Your confidence is based first on living in accordance with God's commands set forth in the Ten Commandments. When you work daily to walk this path with God, it gives you a solid foundation. This faith in God creates a sense of self-worth that can never be broken. God has made sure, and it's written in (*ESV*, Luke 12:6-7), "Are not five sparrows sold for two pennies? And not one of them is forgotten before God. Why, even the hairs of your head are all numbered. Fear not; you are of more value than many sparrows."

Coming back to the exercise I suggest: The exercise must begin with you listing what your doubts are, or ones you often have when performing. Doubt is having uncertainty; you might be indecisive and even choke. You can be confused, not know what the right thing is to do, and hesitate to take action, which leaves you behind; the ball flies right past you into the catcher's mitt. Doubt is thinking too much. Your mind is churning thoughts, and it takes away your ability to focus and perform. This is not your real 'self'. Attachment to something, which is not real, which you can't change, would only aggravate your fear, anxiety, and pain.

You can take care of negative emotions like doubt by taking care of the different interdependent parts of your consciousness which consist of, according to Thich Nhat Hanh:

David L. Angeron

Body and Physical Forms

Feelings

Perceptions

Mental Faculties

Consciousness (P. 46)

All these parts are intimately connected, which connects you further with the outside world. You have to see your being in all the five aspects, and all the five into your one being. There shouldn't be any barrier. The moment a barrier arises, you fall into a false belief. The other thing, which you need to keep in mind, is that you're also not travelling alone in the time and space, impervious to the world around you. You're a life.

You are not only connected to your suffering and joy but also to the others around you, which makes your life limitless. Every part of you becomes limitless when you connect yourself to the super-consciousness, which is God. God harmonizes each part of you. And you're ready to overcome all of your doubts, fear, and dread. You will feel liberated.

Right now, go ahead and take yourself back to those moments where you were not sure what to do, how you were going to do it, or you missed something entirely. List what your doubts and fears were, and any that you have right now about your sports performance, life, and your relationship with God. There's no doubt that you want to transcend those psychological boundaries.

The Greatest Teammate

I have doubts about . . .

Now that you've brought this to the surface, let's give this burden to Jesus as he taught in the New Testament. Pray at this moment, and repeat it every day: Jesus, take my burden of doubt and fear about . . . and fill me with your spirit of power, of peace and the knowing of what I need to do next. I'm walking the path of righteousness and I can hear in my heart God's direction for me. Without a doubt, all those who follow Christ share in this illumination: the light they have received from it, like Christ, they in turn radiate this brightness. Like it's said in (Mark 4:21-23), "And he would say to them: "Since when is the lamp brought in to be put under the bushel basket or under the bed? It's put on the lampstand, isn't it? " After all, there is nothing hidden except to be brought to light, nor anything secreted away that won't be exposed. "1f anyone here has two good ears, use them!" Amen.

> *The voice of truth says, "Do not be afraid!"*
> *And the voice of truth says, "This is for My glory"*
> *Out of all the voices calling out to me*
> *I will choose to listen and believe*
> *I will choose to listen and believe the voice of truth*
> *I will listen and believe, I will listen and believe the voice of truth*
> *I will listen and believe, 'cause Jesus you are the voice of truth*
> *And I will listen to you, you are (Casting Crowns, 2003).*

Even though you gave your best to pray when you were feeling down and faced our doubts, there's more work to be done and it's overcoming fear. In the next chapter, I cover fear, the one thing holding you back from success. There are several easy steps to finally clear the path to success in your life, and I'll cover those next.

Chapter 5
Overcoming Fear

"Courageous"–by Casting Crowns

What is man? A man is born weak and fragile, naked in its natural state, dependent on another human being, for food, for security, for warmth, and yet vulnerable at the same time. The moment he develops his sense and perceptions, he understands all the insults and bullying directed at him or her. He is feeble, lacking physical strength. He eats and works on himself and grows muscles to answer ably to those who agitate him. But these are external features pleasing to the eye. It's ever changing. There's still toil, cold, and heat to face. He learns that his physical appearance decays in idleness. He becomes fearful seeing his own imperfections. He is always fearful for his own safety.

So he strengthens his mind and ignores all the things, which irritate him. He sees the first death of someone close. He comes to know of some higher force working mysteriously all the time. He prays with his innocent and naïve heart. He understands emotions like pain and anger. He understands fear. He understands joy by overcoming those fears: fear of his mortality, fear of his superfluous appearance, fear of his whole flawed being.

What is fear then?

1. Fear is a passion of the soul.
2. Fear is specially a strong emotion.
3. Fear is natural.

Fear implies the presence of an evil which needs an overcoming. It passively builds and transmutes inside your being. So, there is a movement which has a motion and power to either build you or deteriorate you. It also affects your senses depending on how you react to this emotion moving inside of you. Since we're a rational being, we have our own unique conditioning and intelligence at disposal. So we perceive things, good, or bad, according to our own understandings. Based on our own argument and reason, we make things pleasant, painful, agreeable, or dangerous.

Then our souls respond accordingly and allay our fear if there is one. The soul becomes apprehensive of the future if it's threatened by the passion of fear.

Our sense is too busy with the present. It doesn't have time to apprehend what's coming. It can only hope for its future to be good, or to fear a future which is worse. If the object of hope is possible to obtain, then our sense strives towards it in order to achieve it. If it's not possible to overcome or conquer the possible bad, then our sense recoils in fear.

Fear becomes a special emotion when it comes to us through love; the love which connects us with each other. For example, you love your game passionately, but there's a fear of possible future injury lurking inside your head. Or an encounter with a much stronger team is giving you sleepless nights.

If you meditate on your defense mechanism carefully; you wouldn't let the emotions of fear overwhelm you. However, if you avoid those emotions, then your fear would become a nightmarish reality.

Fear is natural. If the opposing force is unusual and sudden, we fear it more. The fear reaches its peak if the opposing force is impossible to avoid. If we find ourselves alone in the face of danger that we can't contain; our fear grows exponentially. A chill passes through us when we see our strength melting away. If I have to make you understand through a metaphor, then fear has the nature of growing like a fire; if unchecked, it will move upward. Fire has the capacity to shrink any vegetation into ashes; likewise, fear can shrink a man's existence. Shame, temptation, anxiety, laziness, all is capable of making our lives miserable and saddening. We must strengthen our soul to avoid things which induce fear in our heart.

Courage is the opposite of fear. One kind of courage is when you expose yourself to danger and confront it head on. The other is when you passively resist the danger. There's another kind of courage where you're calm and composed in the face of danger.

It's such an emotion, which violently brings our attention to the present, whether passively or actively. Our mind and body go completely out of sync. We can't think of anything else. We become quiet for a few moments until we come to understand it. So overcoming a fear requires your attention.

Why self-awareness or self-mastery is important? Fear, like joy and anger, is a strong emotion. It's hard to examine ourselves by keeping ourselves as an observant outsider. We can examine our own thoughts. But, we can't introspect our present. Introspection is always passive in nature, and it is a thought based on the past events. But by being consistent with our thought of the past events, we are continually assessing ourselves at the same time. William James says, 'one doesn't flee because one is afraid; one is afraid because one flees'. The object of your fear is indifferent to you; but you're in very much grip of it. So self-mastery is important.

Making a major life change is scary. As I mentioned before, I too had to face the truth that I wasn't living my best life. I left my responsibilities behind, and worst of all, I left God behind. Luckily, God made us courageous and able to face any adversity and error on our part, giving us the ability to face the issue, correct it, and move on to be a better person, be a Good Samaritan. You can overcome fear by showing compassion.

You were born to perish and experience loss, to feel hope, to long for death and dread it at the same time; worst of all, never to know of your purpose of why you ever existed.

It's not always easy to admit we fear something, and often we pass it off as anxiety, not fear, and we shove it away and bear through the problem. Fear is for the wusses, or so we're told. We tell ourselves whatever the problem or stress; if we don't pay attention to it then we sell ourselves on the idea that it will just go away. We've all done it to some extent because it's the easy way out.

But we're not looking for the easy way out; we're looking for the good and honest way that leads us to real success that last forever. Have you ever thought to yourself after losing a game, "I will just tell the press guys the same stuff about too many injuries and having too many rookies. I just want to go home." That only lasts so long, because you know there are several questionable plays you made that need to be dealt with, not buried. How else will you do better next time? And when the next game comes and you're stressed about the last game and the errors that were never corrected, what are you going to do then?

A common reaction to feeling fear is to become angry and lash out at those closest to us. Men, in particular, are taught that anger is an acceptable way to act and your friends and family let you blow off the steam and assume you'll get over it and everything will be better later. Throwing equipment around, punching holes in walls, yelling at teammates or parents or even unexpressed anger that leads to walking away and keeping the anger trapped inside is all unhealthy, unproductive, hurtful to others and yourself, and most of all it's not a behavior that would please God.

A short-tempered man is a fool and looks foolish. Basically, they are throwing an adult-sized temper tantrum that can hold more consequences. You lose respect, honor, and aren't seen as reliable. "Don't be quick-tempered—that is being a fool" (*TLB*, Ecclesiastes 7:9). It has been advised in (*TLB*, Proverbs 19:11), "A wise man restrains his anger and overlooks insults. This is to his credit." Again in (*TLB*, Proverbs 16:32), "It is better to be slow-tempered than famous; it is better to have self-control than to control an army."

David L. Angeron

We were made to be courageous
We were made to lead the way
We could be the generation
That finally breaks the chains
We were made to be courageous
We were made to be courageous
We were warriors on the front lines
Standing, unafraid (Casting Crowns, 2011)

There is no better example of this kind of restraint, this type of calm and cool-headedness when tempted with anger and the desire for retribution than in Joseph (*NKJV*, Genesis 37:1-50). What's interesting about what's written about Joseph in the Bible is that we get to see his entire life spanning from the favoritism his father bestowed upon him to his brother's trying to kill him, Joseph not giving into temptation and not only forgiving those who wronged him but helping them. Not once did he lose his temper and give into fear of death, loss, inability, failure, or thoughts of retribution.

Get over anger quickly. It's written in The Bible, "If you are angry, don't sin by nursing your grudge. Don't let the sun go down with you still angry—get over it quickly; For when you are angry you give a mighty foothold to the devil" (*TLB*, Ephesians 4:26-27)

We've all seen the guy who's lost his temper. Take a moment right now and think back to a time when you lost your cool, stopped thinking straight and got angry. When was that? Did you throw something? Punch something or someone? Did you deepen your voice and threaten someone? Did you walk off really angry, but never resolved it?

Whichever one you chose to do above, it involved losing your temper and giving into fear. It may not seem like it, but you were scared. The only reason we lash out at people and become angry is because of fear.

A player I knew always seemed to be pretty stable, win or lose. Later in the season I noticed small changes after he didn't perform as well, but it was just a bowed head, cap pulled down lower than usual, and he'd grip everything so tight I thought the bat would splinter under the pressure. But he never said anything or did anything dramatic. Finally, one day, all that pressure that was building inside him blew up and everyone seemed caught off guard. Later that night he was in a car accident and I felt guilty that I hadn't pulled him aside and worked it out with him instead of letting him go blow off the steam on his own. Thankfully, he was okay, and no one was hurt physically, but the lesson is he harbored that disappointment in himself the entire time. After we spoke about what was going on and talked about solutions, he admitted he was afraid of making mistakes, which of course led to more mistakes. The embarrassment and pain of not performing perfectly was so much he got to the point where he didn't know how to deal with it anymore. He exploded in anger and couldn't stop himself until his car did the job for him.

David L. Angeron

Make us courageous
Lord, make us courageous
This is our resolution
Our answer to the call
(Casting Crowns, 2011)

The point is overcoming the fear daily, not letting it build up over time and ignoring it or hoping it will get better tomorrow. Facing up to issues at the moment is okay. First, I tell players it's okay to feel afraid.

Second, humble yourself before God and ask for guidance. Third, turn off the distractions (yes, turn off your phone and sit in a room without a computer or other people) and review what went wrong and begin to think about solutions. This step isn't about "I should have done this" thinking, but "next time, I could do this." If you don't have good answers, it's time to ask those around you that can help. Fourth, keep praying. Fifth, keep working hard and striving for the best.

1. It is okay to feel afraid and feel disappointment.
2. Pray and ask Jesus to take that fear off your shoulders.
3. Turn off your devices and away from distractions. Review what went wrong and think of solutions.
4. Keep praying.
5. Work hard and keep striving for the best.

When the world hands you a load of fear, especially all of a sudden, and you think all is lost, it's hard to think straight. A sudden medical diagnosis that could take your career away, an injury during a tight game, the list goes on. When faced with immediate fears that can overwhelm your thought and emotions, it can seem like there's no way out and it's difficult to feel so out of control.

How can we handle our fears? By believing God's promise to us in, (*NKJV,* Isaiah 41:10), "Fear not, for I am with you; Be not dismayed, for I am your God. I will strengthen you, yes, I will help you, I will uphold you with My righteous right hand."

I've found that in times where there doesn't seem to be a light at the end of the tunnel and fear is deeply rooted, I can uproot the fear and get back into my right mind with right thinking by repeating my favorite and most empowering verses from the Bible. When fearful, remember God. *It's in the Bible* (*NKJV,* Joshua 1:9), "Have I not commanded you? Be strong and of good courage; do not be afraid, nor be dismayed, for the LORD your God *is* with you wherever you go."

Keep the faith. What is there to fear if Christ is with you? *It's in the Bible* (*NKJV,* Matthew 8:26), "But He said to them, "Why are you fearful, O you of little faith?" Then He arose and rebuked the winds and the sea, and there was a great calm"

And my all-time favorite is, "I can do all things through Christ which strengthens me" (*NKJV,* Philippians 4:13).

In The Master Training Guide For Elite Athletes I wrote about taking goals and inspirational quotes and putting them up in your home, your car and your locker.

Many athletes like motivational quotes, and those are great, but there's no glory in success without God. Add a verse that means something special to you, or one you'd like to memorize above the goals you have listed next to your mirror in the bathroom. Memorizing verses can really help when you've found yourself in a bad spot and need help refocus and getting yourself back into the game.

The Greatest Teammate

Take a moment right now to list some of your favorite verses. If you don't have any right now, go back through this book and highlight ones that speak to you and rewrite them here. It may seem like a test to write down or copy the verses here, but the act of doing it will help you memorize the verse quicker. Write the ones you like the most on larger pieces of paper and go around and post them where you'll see them daily. Be sure to have three to five verses at the minimum.

Let the pounding of our hearts cry
We will serve the Lord
We were made to be courageous
And we're taking back the fight
We were made to be courageous
And it starts with us tonight
The only way we'll ever stand
Is on our knees with lifted hands
Make us courageous
Lord, make us courageous
This is our resolution
Our answer to the call
We will love our wives and children
We refuse to let them fall
We will reignite… (Casting Crowns, 2013).

What is a happy life then? The most important thing is that it has been realized through the will of God. Second, it's having a mind that is independent, elevated, and fearless. A mind that exists beyond the reach of fear and of desire that regards honor as the only good and shame as the only evil, and everything else as the trivial collection of things which come and go. I leave you with a beautiful verse from (*ESV,* Ephesians 6:10-18), "Finally, be strong in the Lord and in the strength of his might. Put on the whole armor of God, that you may be able to stand against the schemes of the devil. For we do not wrestle against flesh and blood, but against the rulers, against the authorities, against the cosmic powers over this present darkness, against the spiritual forces of evil in the heavenly places. Therefore, take up the whole armor of God that you may be able to withstand in the evil day, and having done all, to stand firm. Stand therefore, having fastened on the belt of truth, and having put on the breastplate of righteousness ..." And one from (*ESV,* Philippians 1:27), "Only let your manner of life be worthy of the gospel of Christ, so that whether I come and see you or am absent, I may hear of you that you are standing firm in one spirit, with one mind striving side by side for the faith of the gospel." Amen.

The Greatest Teammate

Chapter 6
Commitment & Motivation

"God is Enough"-by Lecrae

The first step to becoming God's teammate is making a commitment and being motivated to stick with that commitment. To be happy in life, you don't need material things; you don't need approval from others. All you need is God. God is enough.

Read these great lyrics by Lecrae for his song, "God is Enough."

> *Used to want a lot of things*
> *All the stuff that's on TV*
> *Education, cars, and clothes*
> *Fashion lights and jewelry*
> *(Focused on the wrong stuff)*
> *Now I got my eyes on you*
> *And now I know that*
> *God is enough-nough*
> *God is enough-nough*
> *God is enough-nough*
> *You are enough-nough (Lecrae, 2010)*

We can make a silent vow and commit to it secretly. Let all that perish! Let us set aside these vain and empty ambitions. Let us concentrate exclusively on the search for the truth. Life is full of misery; death is closer to us than life. It may suddenly carry us off. Think about the state in which your soul departs your body. It could be our biggest motivator. It makes us introspect on things which we have neglected here. We commit not to negligence but to the alertness of mind. Can we commit ourselves to the conformity of God's will?

Let us put aside the idea of death for a minute. It is not for nothing, that a sea of humanity has belief in God and his son Jesus. It's not an empty significance. What kind of commitment has sustained this belief for time immemorial? Is it enough motivation to save our soul from being corrupted and be a part of secular hopes? Jesus would not have done all that for us, in quality and in quantity, if with the body's death the soul's life was also destroyed. Still, we don't hesitate second to abandon our faith in God, even after a minor setback. Commit ourselves wholly to God and life.

But wait a moment. Secular successes are pleasant. They have no small sweetness of their own. Our motivation is not to be deflected from them by a superficial decision; for it would be a disgrace to return to the bad faith. Bad faith means we lose all hope in ourselves too. It is a considerable thing to set out to obtain preference for high office. And what worldly prize could be more desirable? We have plenty of influential friends.

It's easy to get trapped in the whirlpool of life with friends and everyone on social media pushing for you to think "their way" and making it easy to stop being yourself; questioning what you are told or see, remembering your goals and values and simply going along with the crowd. Time passes by. You 'delayed turning to the Lord' and postponed 'from day to day'. You have postponed the fact that every day you're dying within yourself. At the same time you're not content and longed for the happy life, but were afraid of the place where it has to be found, and fled from it at the same time instead of seeking it. You believe that by hoarding material things would be enough to motivate your life towards completeness. Have you found anything worth possessing that can nourish your soul?

Where does commitment fail to deliver? We have our mind to blame for it, when we fill our mind with corpulent waste.

The affections of your mind remain preoccupied with the same memory. They are not happening on their own. You must have experienced them in the past or desire to experience the moment the first opportunity presents itself. You have visualized all the vile things which could corrupt your soul, instead of visualizing the techniques of your game. Now it holds immense power over you. You have lost your bearings and are floating in the void from where only a hard fall is the only return.

I am presenting a situation to you and asking you to look at yourself objectively. Are you glad or sad to look at your past 'self' when you had those relapses? Were you afraid or maybe even embarrassed?

Physical pain would pass away, but the mind which has gone astray on recklessness would be hard to reconcile with. Your mind deceives you into thinking that it had slipped your mind or that it was a onetime mistake. Commit now to reverse this and make your mind glad by clearing the knots of your mind.

Commit to the fact that God has commanded you without question to abstain 'from the lust of the flesh and the lust of the eyes and the ambition of the world' (*NIV*, 1 John 2:16). God has advised you to adopt a better way of life than he has allowed (*NIV*, 1 Cor. 7: 38). And He also has granted you the strength to fight with the illusory pleasure. The illusory image in your soul is not strong enough to fight with the strength with which the Lord has equipped you. A false dream is not devoted enough to follow it with careless abandon without looking at the reality of your life, which demands attention. Will the reality not smack at your face when you're awake? It will, if you have taken the words of God as the rightful motivator, "When the righteous cry for help, the Lord hears and delivers them out of all their troubles. The Lord is near to the brokenhearted and saves the crushed in spirit. Many are the afflictions of the righteous, but the Lord delivers him out of them all. He keeps all his bones; not one of them is broken" (*ESV,* Psalm 34:17-20). Does it not motivate you towards your true 'self'? There shouldn't be any difference between your waking state and your dream state. There shouldn't be any difference between your mind and your body. Each one of them should work as an organic whole.

You will understand if you apply your reason to it, when wide-awake, you must resist digressing thoughts, and would remain unmoved if the actual reality presents itself. Surely reason does not shut down as the eyes close. It can hardly fall asleep with the bodily senses. For if that were so, how could it come about that often in sleep we resist and, mindful of our avowed commitment and adhering to it.

We give no assent to such seductions of life. You would surely feel the difference that your conscience is at peace and there is no rift within the soul. In (Matthew 16:24), "If anyone would come after me, let him deny himself and take up his cross and follow me. For whoever would save his life will lose it, but whoever loses his life for my sake will find it. For what will it profit a man if he gains the whole world and forfeits his soul? Or what shall a man give in return for his soul? For the Son of Man is going to come with his angels in the glory of his Father, and then he will repay each person according to what he has done. Truly, I say to you, there are some standing here who will not taste death until they see the Son of Man coming in his kingdom." What could be more motivating than this that by forfeiting your life

The Greatest Teammate

only you could preserve it? Of course, it should not be taken in literal terms.

But It takes discipline and focus to stay committed and motivated to stay on the good path and stand up for what you believe in. What does it take to get up every day and feel motivated to the highest extent possible? How can you stay committed to your faith in God every single day when you're so busy? It's easy to say it takes discipline and focus, but what does that really entail? It entails training our mind. Before that, we have to understand how it works?

Much of what I speak and write about in The Mental Training Guide is valuable, easy-to-use techniques to stay on track. Creating goals and implementing them into a daily schedule, making it part of your daily routine is one. When you fall off track, you immediately pick up where you left off, and as soon as you noticed that your focus and motivation shifted. You look down and see your shoelaces are undone; you bend down in the moment and tie them up, not wait until tomorrow or when they are ratty and have to be replaced. So why not do the same when you see that you're cheating on how many reps you're doing or not taking time during your morning and evening to pray? You thought about it, so there's no better time than right now to take care of.

There's another side of discipline, where you need a swift kick to get back in line. And the discipline we receive is an indication of love from our Father. *It's in the Bible*, (*NIV,* Hebrews 12:5-11), "My son, do not make light of the Lord's discipline, and do not lose heart when he rebukes you, because the Lord disciplines those he loves, and he punishes everyone he accepts as a son. Endure hardship as discipline;

God is treating you as sons. For what son is not disciplined by his father?

"Moreover, we have all had parents who disciplined us and we respected them for it. How much more should we submit to the Father of our spirits and live! Our parents disciplined us for a little while as they thought best; but God disciplines us for our good, that we may share in his holiness. No discipline seems pleasant at the time, but painful. Later on, however, it produces a harvest of righteousness and peace for those who have been trained by it."

When we were kids, certainly there was discipline doled out after we ran straight through the house, dirty shoes making muddy tracks on the floor, and we still hadn't finished our chores from yesterday. Today, we've got taxes to pay on time and a family that needs us. The hard lessons learned as a kid, when we didn't have a weekend free to play and did chores instead, were there to teach us to be responsible. Penalties for not filing taxes on time, jail time if you lie or cheat or being shamed on social media for saying something not appropriate. These are all disciplines that come down on us so we can learn from the mistakes and not make them again. We're being shown the correct way, and at first the consequences are minor, like losing a weekend to relax and have time with friends. When you keep ignoring the discipline and take the lazy way, the consequences become more severe, and the fault lies entirely with you.

The Greatest Teammate

God is there to discipline you, to keep you on the right track. Keep the faith and know He has your best interest and wants you to succeed, but you first have to commit to doing well and changing follow His word. When you commit, the possibilities of success and joy are endless. It's in the Bible "Commit your way to the Lord; trust in him, and he will act." Psalm 37:5-9, "He will make your vindication shine like the light, and the justice of your cause like the noonday. Be still before the Lord, and wait patiently for him; do not fret over those who prosper in their way, over those who carry out evil devices. Refrain from anger . . ."

It may seem that you have to wait for your turn at success, and while you're waiting, watch those that don't care, are talented and don't work hard or even cheat to gain success. Patience and staying committed to God and doing good works will pay off, and your faith and continual motivation to do good will be rewarded.

David L. Angeron

MOTIVATION IN SPORTS

I ask you to think of an athlete who has dominated your favorite sport, such as Lance Armstrong, Rafael Nadal, Tiger Woods, or Serena Williams. John Lester is a survivor. All are talented, but they are also known for their incredible work ethic and drive. What drives them to such finesse, where you just marvel at the magic they spin on the ground. They must be motivating themselves with something. Without motivation, talented athletes do not reach their full potential. And athletes who are not particularly talented can achieve a great deal of success with strong desire and motivation.

Their commitment stemmed from their love of the game and the satisfaction they derived from working toward their goals. They're persistent competitors. What drives them to excel? For an athlete to sustain hard training, compete aggressively, and focus their energies toward specific goals is indeed a challenge. It's one thing to develop motivation when things are going well; it's a whole new challenge to keep the motivation running in times of adversity or during the off-season.

Motivation is influenced by many factors. There is no quick fix or simple solution. Rather than focus on simple how-to approaches, which tend to oversimplify, we should focus on understanding *why* athletes are motivated. Motivation is unique to each one of them. Some are motivated by an hour of running. Some are motivated by mental imagery. Some excels in adversity. They push hard when they are down.

Motivation is not intrinsic to you. It's the job of the coach to observe you minutely when you play, when you're off the steam, and offer you solutions. You can also look at a few factors, like the choices you have made. Why are you playing this game? Okay, you have chosen baseball? Why? Why did you choose to be a pitcher? So your choice is an important determiner of your motivation. Next is effort. If you're pursuing your own area of a chosen field, how much effort you're putting into it. What you do off the field is as important as you are on the field? The final one is persistence. Motivation level can be seen in how long athletes persist at striving to attain their goals, even in the face of adversity and obstacles.

There are several myths attached to it. That motivation is attached to athletes' personalities. It can't be developed. It's also not some vaccine shot where you take one and you're ready to go. Through punishment and rewards, we can set the button of motivation on. Carrot and stick policy would surely backfire. Motivation is first intrinsic.

What do athletes need from sport? Evidence from a variety of sources suggests that athletes seek to fulfill four primary needs: to have fun and experience stimulation and excitement, to feel accepted and belong to a group which you can say at the most basic level is your social needs, to exercise control and autonomy, and to feel competent. Why do they indulge in sports in the first place? They indulge in sports to develop their skill set, and also to have fun.

Sport is much more enjoyable when athletes find practice activities stimulating, challenging, and exciting. It doesn't matter whether the practice is intense and highly structured. The moment it becomes monotonous, an athlete will lose steam. The drills are either boring or beyond your skill level. You often appear antagonistic to the coach, who constantly threatens and administers discipline.

For a change, play something else. Play basketball just for fun and take it as an opportunity to bond with the teammates. The coach has failed to realize that most of these kids wanted to play basketball for fun in a way that is enjoyable, not to do drills and calisthenics all day. Nor do they want to be yelled at.

YOU'RE SOMEONE'S TEAMMATE, TOO

There are responsibilities as a teammate and that means you also have to take responsibility for your role as a teammate. This means lending someone a hand, encouraging them, speaking the truth about their performance and need for changes. A lot of psychologists and counselors kick around the phrase "Courageous Conversations" and that means having talks with teammates, friends, families and coaches that take courage because you know they could be tough talks. We all have emotions, unchecked and unhampered, they can get in the way of good, honest talks with people. When you are angry with someone for their continually bad performance, it's not going to help when you yell at them about doing better. How can they do better? Are you offering solutions or just spouting off a bunch of "I can't stand it when you…" or "If you'd just be more aware…" The issue is you're not sharing with them how to be more aware; real techniques that could help them perform better. And you may not have those answers, so it's useless to get angry and spout off. You're actually helping to bury the guy even deeper than he already is at that moment. We are our own worst enemies and rarely need to be reminded of our mistakes and buried further underneath them. You want your teammate to perform better? Then lend them a hand up and out of the hole they're in.

There's no one harder on us . . . than ourselves. When someone comes up and yells at you, it may motivate some players to snap their minds back into the game, but generally being yelled at doesn't truly solve the root cause. You'll find yourself back in the same spot of either being yelled at or yelling, and nothing yet has changed.

ALWAYS COME TO THE FIELD WITH SOLUTIONS

That also means, come to every problem, and every person, with at least two- three solutions. Otherwise, you simply don't care enough and it shows to everyone. People that come to complain or say nothing at all and fail silently and slowly either look like complainers or failures. You don't want to be either one, so consider solutions and actively seek out those who can help you choose the best solution, implement it and stick to it daily.

In my practice of the Mental Master Method, I teach Play the Next Pitch. It requires you to consider the mental side of the game and change your thoughts so you can leave behind the last play that didn't go so well and refocus on the next play. Same goes for choosing God as your teammate. When you turn to God, when you're down, He leads you to go higher, to lose your burdens and regrets and start over, not looking back but forward to the next pitch.

Just like you train for your sport, you train with God through prayer. As Jesus said in Matthew 6:6, But whenever you pray, go into your room and shut the door and pray to your Father who is in secret; and your Father who sees in secret will reward you.

Being in secret means that your conversation with God is just between you and Him, and that you are seeking His direction, not your own. He knows what's in your heart already; you don't have to explain it or plead it out. Going into your closet means quieting your overthinking brain that questions everything, judges everything, and thinks it knows everything. You don't know everything, only God does, so get quiet and listen.

The Greatest Teammate

This act of going into your closet and praying is in line with more of the Mental Master Methods I write and talk about often, and I refer to as mental imagery. I'll go further into this method and how it relates to prayer. Right now there's one to spur you up.

Lazy people do not have good judgment. *It's in the Bible*, Proverbs (*TLB*, 26:13-16), "The lazy man won't go out and work. 'There might be a lion outside!' he says. He sticks to his bed like a door to its hinges! Here's a serious lesson for the lazy, courtesy of an ant. *It's in the Bible*, Proverbs (*TLB*, 6:6-11), "Take a lesson from the ants, you lazy fellow. Learn from their ways and be wise! For though they have no king to make them work, yet they labor hard all summer, gathering food for the winter. But you—all you do is sleep. When will you wake up? 'Let me sleep a little longer!' Sure, just a little more! And as you sleep, poverty creeps upon you like a robber and destroys you; it attacks you in full armor."

I would leave you with the beautiful lyrics of "God is Enough". Listen to it and find motivation.

Lord is my Sheppard, I shall not want
Takes away my fears, You restore my soul
Off into the sky, To dead and Christ arise
To be with You forever, see with the clearest eyes
Push my inner thirst to somethin' more in life
No money, cars, relationships compare to joy in Christ
Love to work that selfish ways, that like to flirt will self-destruct
No need to strut, know what I want, know how to get it, but my God's enough!

David L. Angeron

Who left His heavenly home
Never did anything wrong
They crucified Him on
On a tree, there He made
It was crazy how it set the stage
For His resurrection from the grave, that gets me amazed
You can be the fliest man
With a hundred-grand in your hand
Swag right, sag tight
And a Gucci fan
You can be the richest, be the smartest, be the hardest, all of that
But I guarantee before i die they all are fallin' flat

God is enough
God is enough
God is enough
You are enough
Never too much
More than enough
God is enough
You are enough for me (Lecrae, 2010)

The Greatest Teammate

Chapter 7
GOALS AND GOD'S WILL

"MOVE"–FLAME

By following God's plan, you're on your way to the next step of a relationship with God. If you listen closely, God will speak to you and give you directions. So many people develop their own plan, then when it fails, they ask for God's help. Why would God want to help with a plan that he didn't create for you? God's Will is the key. Speak with him and listen. When the Lord tells me to move, I move!

> *This verse by Flame hits it perfectly.*
> *Now when the Lord tells me move, I move*
> *Anything He wants me to yeah I do*
> *But if ain't of the Lord then I won't move*
> *It's because the Spirit lives*
> *So I still show your love*
> *When He tells me I move*
> *Talking about obedience (2010)*

We need God's wisdom, his intellect to achieve our desired goals. If any one of you lacks wisdom, let him ask God who gives generously and without any reproach (*ESV,* James 1:5). We can expect only natural good from God, because he can't will otherwise. The will of God resides with Him in natural perfection. The divine will is His essence. It has its own existence. For when we say God exists, we don't imply any relation external to it. Every Goal of ours is inclined towards an end. If you're down with an injury, your only end is to get back on your feet. God wills things apart from Himself for its own sake. His own goodness suffices the will.

We are only certain of the will of God concerning the past. We attribute our failings to the act of God. Oh, had it not rained, we would have won. We use it as a means to hide our own shame. At the same time, we attribute the good thing in our life to our own hard work. We fail to realize that everything that has happened, whatever it may be, is in accordance with the will of the almighty Father.

The future also, whatever it may contain, once it has come about, will have come about in conformity with the will of God (Weil, P.218). We can neither add to nor take from this conformity. We can't just push our desire impossibly high and strive for it at any cost. By doing that we're denying the eternal reality of God's word, "For it is God who works in you, both to will and to work for his good purpose" (*ESV,* Philippians 2:13).

Now how are we going to accomplish it, whatever it may be, our object of desire into an established fact. What would we do if we can't accomplish it? Should we treat it with utter resignation? I don't think we should. Should we accept it? I think acceptance is a weak word. With acceptance, we don't have any recourse but to submit ourselves to the situation. We desire in such a way that everything has happened should have happened, and nothing else. Not because what has happened is good, but God has purposed it to be good. This should be our belief and obedience to the will of God, which is absolute and holy.

But a man wishes to live happily. When it comes to seeing clearly what it is that makes life happy, they grope for the light. Yes, you have to invest more energy in striving towards a more difficult goal. You take unnecessary stress. You may hit a wrong turn on the road. Now the road on which you have set yourself is now taking you in the opposite direction. The swiftness of your effort is now putting resistance. What should you do?

The Greatest Teammate

You must first establish what you seek to gain; then you must search for the right way to take you there most naturally, and during the journey itself, provided you are on the correct path, you will come to know how many small goals you have put behind each day, and how much closer you are to the goal and your natural desire still sustain you on the arduous journey.

Now, if you wander aimlessly, having no guide and following only the noise of men calling you in different directions, your life will be spent in making errors. You have got a life of little enough span even if you should work night and day you wouldn't achieve what you have set out for. So let us determine both the goal and the road we will take, and let us have an experienced guide which is God, who has the intelligence of any territory we can think of entering.

We need our own intelligence to understand this for our Goals to achieve. Goal is not just an end which we can quantify in success and failure, or happiness for that matter. Our Goal should be to acquire wisdom to align ourselves with God. Life can become bearable and worth living by just refining that wisdom. But, we have conditioned as such into a rat race where survival for the fittest is the maxim to live. Each one of us is at everyone's throat. We're running at breakneck speed. We hear the exhortations, 'work hard', 'give your best', along the way. Our whole effort goes in looking over our shoulder, sheltering ourselves from the onslaught of ever-changing social order. A trend in social media has the capacity to alter our thought process. A one-line tweet could wreak havoc with our lives, could define anybody. Failure, success everything exists outside of us. What defines us? How can we define our Goals then? We're not equipped mentally to the ever-changing temporal, spatial landscape of our true reality. Our own spaces are not defined. Where do we exist, exactly? Are we just a simulation? Culture has a new meaning. We cancel everything, which doesn't suit our herd mentality, which doesn't fit in our ecosystem. What is our goal then?

Okay, you have progressed a lot. But, there's something artificial about it. You're living a pretense. Please stop for a moment to search your 'self', to examine yourself in a different way. Subject yourself to an ethical and moral prism of a higher consciousness. Our 'self' is hollow. How can you connect with your 'self'? What will drive you to the shore when your mind is not at ease? If anything, you want to cancel is, cancel all the noises, which are immediate, which are intimate, which are close. The origin of a contented life starts with elevating your thought to God's will. It doesn't mean you have to feel contempt for yourself. Contempt is a very negative emotion. It will only harm you. Self-contempt is the sign of defeatism. You have worked hard. You have strived for Goals befitting your status. All you have to do is to change the direction towards something we can say, 'it was an honorable achievement'. Put your effort into it. Again, let me remind you; don't let yourself get bewitched or overwhelmed by it.

Rise, breathe deeply, and scale the slope in one mighty breath. That would be noble. Yes, you can do it. Nourish your spirit with something noble. What is honorable and what is shameful? So, what is a good goal? The good goal is the knowledge of life and according to whose will we're living it. What is a bad goal? The bad goal is the ignorance where your effort goes in vain. A good goal is not misplaced, empty, or superfluous. A good goal resides with God's will.

The Greatest Teammate

At first, it seems difficult to let go of our wants and desires. We definitely want a nice new car and a fancy place to live, but those are the rewards of living in God's Word first. After giving ourselves over to the Lord, we realize we don't even care about the cars, the jewelry and the status, and find our greatest success is given by God, and enjoyed in praising His name. The feeling of genuine success, real joy and accomplishment, comes only with living out God's Will. Everything else we push humanly will never compare to that feeling of having Jesus at your side and knowing you're on the right side, never any fears or worries to cut down your success because God gave them to you, rewarding you for walking beside Him and obeying His Word.

So, how do you obey His Word? How do you hear the Lord? What is God's plan for you, anyway? And how do I turn those into my goals? In order to move forward in a meaningful way, you must tackle all of these questions within yourself and get the answers.

A verse that helps is from (*NRSV,* Matthew 21: 22),"Whatsoever you ask for in prayer with faith, and you will receive." Let's break this down into tangible tasks that you can faithfully do daily in order to hear God's guidance. If you do something in 'good faith' it means you are doing it with honesty and sincerity of intention. Basically, it equates to being honest with your feelings and really means what you so say and do. Instead of the attitude of rolling your eyes over what you must do to get something, it's a sincere attitude that reveals your being true.

In good faith, we turn our thoughts to God and pray. Prayer is filled with gratitude that God is good and is there for us; acknowledging there is only one God and that we only serve Him (not money, not fame, not the devil's temptations); share our feelings and needs that day (ask for forgiveness, ask for advice or a sign so you know where to go and what to do and what to say, ask for strength to obey) and finally, listen.

'Why are you hanging back? Are you afraid of the dust and grime of the toil? No, you shouldn't be afraid of anything when your virtue is pure and constant in spite of everything. It's there because you have acquired the knowledge of life, the art of recognizing things human and divine. This is the supreme good: if you understand the wisdom of God, you are beginning to be a partner with God. You say: 'How do I reach that state?

The Greatest Teammate

We have come again to the question what is the will of God? It means, and how we can reach the point of conforming ourselves to it completely. I will tell you what I think about this.

We have to distinguish between three domains. First domain is absolutely independent of us; it includes all the accomplished facts in the whole universe at the moment. In this domain, everything happens in accordance with the will of God at the purest level. Since everything is happening outside of us, like that reed flowing under the water and a small amphibian which has clung itself to it. And with accepting this beauty, we also accept all the sufferings. In other words, we must feel the reality and presence of God through all external things, without exception, as clearly as our hand feels the touch.

The second domain is placed under the rule of the will. It includes the things that are close to our own natural being, close, easily recognized by our sense and perception. We can make a choice. If the temperature is at its peak, we can skip the run and choose to work out indoors.

The third domain is where we experience the presence of God just because it's written in (*ESV,* Matthew 6:10), "Your kingdom come, your will be done, on earth as it's in heaven." We deserve to experience it. It's also not entirely independent of us. This is the eternal Goal where our presence is welcomed. How can we prepare for it?

Praying first thing in the morning, even before your feet hit the floor and your morning push-ups are out of the way, is the only way to start your day. Take a moment and use all the elements listed above. If it's too much to remember with brain fog, then write it down and have it next to you in bed, or better yet write it above your head on the ceiling—that will remind you that you desire an honorable life. The prerequisite for an honorable life is the honorable actions that you can apply on your present state—not thinking about the past, nor thinking about the future. Don't you laugh at a person who is crying over the lack of opportunities because population has risen, opportunities have shrunk that he wishes he would have born a thousand years earlier so life would have been easier, or he should have born a thousand years from now, because after apocalypse opportunities would be plenty. You exist inside of time. Time is not external to you. You have no say over it. You have been tossed into the moment. How will you fill them with legit desires? Fretting over your place on earth is wasting your effort in the wrong direction. Your pessimism if there's any can be swayed if you hope to be swayed by prayers.

There's something, which is larger than us. It's determined and fixed by a mighty, which is beyond our comprehension. It is right when you say your necessity drives your will. But, it has its own limitations. Sometimes the unconquerable chain of events subdues our will. It has subdued our ancestors. Ask about any pandemic. Our power and immense intelligence suddenly look puny and small. And don't you think you would ask someday when did you reach your goal when you're always travelling? When you're travelling, take this dictum for your road, 'There's no journey without an end'. Pray and live a life with the blessings of God. The blessed life consists of right actions which require an obedient mind. Right action is not sluggish as it will not be driven by our secondary necessities. Right action will be voluntary. It will have a life and motion. Far from the fear of pain, it will have natural movement.

The Greatest Teammate

This is the movement of infants, how they fall and rise on their feel to walk, eventually. Every time the infant test its strength before it slumps down on the floor. How come you lose the capacity of looking at your weaknesses and strength when you grow up? Even an animal has the capacity to thrust its leg upward when it falls on its back. Have you seen an overturned insect? It relentlessly tries to get back on its feet. There's single-minded zeal to it. Can you understand now the wisdom of God? You just have to look around. Your goal will become clear.

After you've said your prayer, stay in that moment of connecting with your Father and silence your thoughts in order to hear. When I say "hear" that means receiving a message no matter what form it comes in. Your Father communicates with you in so many ways, so it's important that you are aware and looking for God in all things. God speaks through other people, comforts you with the love and attention from your pet and many times a solution come our way and all we had to do was keep the faith, and the situation works out in our favor without us saying or doing anything. That's how God works!

With a clear way to pray, it's time to pray about setting goals. *It's in the Bible*, (*TLB*, Luke 14:28-31), "Suppose one of you wants to build a tower. Will he not first sit down and estimate the cost to see if he has enough money to complete it? For if he lays the foundation and is not able to finish it, everyone who sees it will ridicule him, saying, 'This fellow began to build and was not able to finish.' Or suppose a king is about to go to war against another king. Will he not first sit down and consider whether he is able with ten thousand men to oppose the one coming against him with twenty thousand?"

Is it possible for us then to associate our Goal with the will of God and extended to spiritual things? Yes, it is possible. Our spirit rises and falls as we're not an independent agent following our goals in isolation.

The Greatest Teammate

There are so many factors involved other than our own being, for example, our family. Sometimes events unfold above the threshold of time. Instead of complaining, say positively, sometimes you're tossed about and events unfold below the threshold of time. Your spirit is still intact as it acts in conformity with the will of God.

What do I mean by this implicit conformity, which dwells inside the unconscious of your mind? We must detach ourselves from the past and the future. We have to cast aside all other desires for the sake of our desire for eternal life, but we should desire eternal life itself without any attachment.

That's why I talk about the unconscious, which is the heritage of our mind. We built this heritage so that it would help our generation to come. Our mind becomes so resilient, and it wouldn't even attach itself to the detachment. We have to think of eternal life as one thinks of water when dying of thirst.

If we agree to God's entry, He enters. We cannot bind our will today for tomorrow; we cannot make a pact with Him that tomorrow he will take possession of our problems and relieve us of our pain. We have to give consent for the Kingdom to come.

That's why God has asked to desire the simplest of things, like bread. Bread is vital for survival. It humbles us when we receive it when we're hungry. We become disheartened easily when we're unable to fulfill our goals. Bread doesn't dishearten us. Bread is a necessity for us. We need energy. At the most basic level, if our energy is not daily renewed, we become feeble and incapable of movement. Besides actual food, in the literal sense of the word, all incentives are sources of energy for us. Please try to understand that bread is the metaphor for money, ambition, decorations, celebrity hood, power, our loved ones. . . . Everything that puts us into the path of our Goal is like bread.

Right now, if I ask you, can you list below some God-centered goals you can do every day to enable you to hear 'God's Will' for you? For example: My goal is to create my own acronym of priorities to keep me focused and faithful, and I want to really feel that I have it right according to God's Will.

Go ahead and list five God-centered goals below.

It is wise to have a goal in mind. It's in the Bible, (*TLB*, Proverbs 13:16), "A wise man thinks ahead; a fool doesn't and even brags about it!" As we set our goals and live in God's name daily, we fight to keep our minds and our speech clean. Not only does this honor God, it makes you an honorable person who people inherently trust and respect. Have you ever felt deep respect and trust in a person who curses a lot, speaks badly about others and really isn't that funny after listening to their dirty jokes that degrade others? No, you don't. None of us really trust or respect these people, and if you've ever been tempted to hang out with them, you probably noticed you slipped and speak like them. Did it bring you more success? I guarantee it didn't, and most people saw you as a fool, even if they laughed uncomfortably along with you.

If you didn't add it before, add a goal to have a clean mouth and a clean mind and a clean heart that's free from negativity, sickness, and harm to others, and anything unlike God, Good. What should our speech be like? What should be our usual way of talking? It's in the Bible, Colossians 4:6, NIV. "Let your conversation be always full of grace . . . so that you may know how to answer everyone."

The Greatest Teammate

God asks us to rid ourselves of foul language. It's in the Bible, (*NIV*, Colossians 3:8), "But now you must rid yourselves of all such things as these: anger, rage, malice, slander, and filthy language from your lips."

"Dirty stories, foul talk, and coarse jokes—these are not for you. Instead, remind each other of God's goodness and be thankful!" (*TLB*, Ephesians 5:4).

The words we use influence others. It's in the Bible, (*NIV*, 1 Timothy 4:12), "Don't let anyone look down on you because you are young, but set an example for the believers in speech, in life, in love, in faith and in purity."

Now that kind words and thoughts are part of your goals, it's time to really dig into the goals and get the process going. Praying is good, but it must be followed by action!

In The Mental Training Guide, I taught about creating goals and how to stick with those goals daily. There is not a day that goes by where you aren't reading your goals and actively trying to reach them. The simplest and most effective ways to accomplish this task it to actively engage in working with your goals first thing in the morning and it's the last thing you think about at night as you thank God for such a great day, no matter how hard you worked and what obstacles you faced. You wouldn't be successful if you hadn't faced those challenges, so be grateful for them.

Active engagement with your goals begins with writing them down and posting them up in strategic places, like where your Bible verses are next to the bathroom mirror. On the inside of your front door is an important place. Make sure it's bright and bold enough so you can take a second and read them, not skim over them, but really feel that desire to stick with your goals because you know that it serves God and serves those around you, which in turn, serves you and your family. Humility is the trait you must develop in order to serve. Humility consists of knowing that in this world the whole soul, our ego, the supernatural part of the soul, is subject to time and to the vicissitudes of change. It must be accepted as an event that would come about only in conformity with the will of God.

With all things, it is always what comes to us from outside, freely and as a gift from heaven, which we're not consciously seeking, that brings us pure joy. It is a possibility that real good can only come from outside us. Our own effort plays its part unconsciously. We put an effort into better ourselves. Do we have the sole ability to make something out of us which is better than our own being? Only God is the creator. Thus, while putting in effort, we shouldn't expect an immediate result. That would be despairing if we achieve no tangible outcome at the outset, but in perseverance, the gift comes from outside out of nowhere and we marvel at the presence of God.

Now I'm praying for his grace
That every time I would speak in the schools
In the mall, on the job, on the streets
This is how it's gotta be I'm talkin' about obedience
Fearing God, not man, that is the ingredient
Yes I know you can relate
Some of y'all are shackin' up
Time for you to move it out
Get your clothes, back it up (Flame, 2010).

The Greatest Teammate

Chapter 8
Prayer and Imagery

"I Can Only Image"—By Mercy Me

CHAPTER 8: PRAYER AND IMAGERY

INSPIRATIONAL SONG: "I CAN ONLY IMAGINE" BY: MERCY ME

Through prayer we secretly entreat our pleas to God, through prayer we raise our mind to God, through prayer we bare our heart to God, through prayer God thus takes possession of us and grants His mercy and grace. Through prayer, God reciprocates with his loving gaze. According to (*DRA*, Psalm. 9:38), "The Lord has heard the desire of the poor." It can be said, prayer is desire. Through prayer, we surrender ourselves to God in order to unite with Him. This union with God is guided by love. Since we're rational beings and we have been told to use our reason. Is it unreasonable to deny love and affection? St. Augustine says, "Prayer is a petition." He writes about his mother, where his mother beseeches the Lord for her son's salvation. "No indeed, Lord, of course you were there and were hearing her petition" (1998, P. 98). He believes when we desire something, then God hears them before they put up a prayer, according to the verses of (*DRA,* Isaiah. 65:24), "And it shall come to pass, that before they call, I will hear."

Even if you have perceived hell, don't forget to send your petition to the lord. Make a resolve and go on. I ask you to go on a great while, even when the flames reach out to you. Go on, even when you're torn into pieces. A thought would come to your mind that you must retreat. But you go on. Look, you're already halfway through. You have already challenged many setbacks. All you have to do is not let prayer slip from your heart.

Prayer is necessary in a way that we may make our needs known to the Lord to whom we pray. For we pray not that we may change the will of God. Actually, prayer is a way of looking back at our desired necessities objectively that we may recognize Him as the author of our goods. "I will pray with the spirit, I will pray also with the understanding" (*DRA,* 1 Corinthians 14:15).

If you believe in Socrates' words that we should ask the gods for nothing else but that they should grant us good things. He knows what is good for us. But we must be wary of what we ask. Because we know many riches have come to an evil end. Honors have ruined many.

Marriages based on lust have wrecked the family. There are certain goods which we cannot ill-use, because they cannot have an evil result. When we pray, as in (*DRA*, Psalm 118:35), "Lead me into the path of Thy commandments. For this same I have desired." We cannot know by ourselves what we ought to pray for, "the Spirit," or to inspire us with holy desires, He makes us ask for what is right. Hence our Lord said (*DRA*, John 4:24) that God is a spirit, and those who adore Him must adore in spirit and in truth. God so invites us to take good things that we may approach to them not by the steps of the body, but by pious desires and devout prayers.

We seek what we ask for in prayer. But we should not actively seek for material things, for it is written in (*DRA*, Matthew 6:33): "Seek ye ... first the kingdom of God, and His justice: and all these things shall be added unto you." Let me clarify that it is not unbecoming for anyone to desire for a livelihood. You can desire to be clothed that befits your status. You can desire for your welfare. Accordingly, we ought to pray that we may keep these things if we have them, and if we don't have the sufficient goods we may gain possession of them. Thus we say all our humility: "Give us this day our daily bread."

Then we should proceed to fulfill what has been asked of us that "Pray one for another, that you may be saved" (*DRA*, James 5:16). When we pray we should desire good things not only for ourselves but also for others: for this is essential to the love, which we owe to our neighbor, to our teammates, and to our family. You pray according to your own necessity. Like if it's winning an important match. But you can't accomplish it alone. Brotherhood and charity urge you to pray for your teammate as well.

The Greatest Teammate

We say 'Our Father' and not 'My Father,' 'Give us' and not 'Give me'. It can be derived that prayers of a multitude are more easily heard, and the grace of God is also multiplied. You must have understood by now that the Lord's prayer should be rightly desired so that the prayer teaches you not only to ask but also direct all your affections. The end of affection is God. We can show it in two ways: first, by willing the glory of God, secondly, by willing to enjoy His glory. Hence the affection is reciprocated on its own. We love God in Himself while we love ourselves in God. If you remember the first petition which is expressed as: "Hallowed be Thy name," and the second: "Thy kingdom come". Prayer is offered up to God, not that we may draw Him to us, but that we may enjoy in ourselves the confidence to ask His good. Therefore, we say: "Who art in heaven."

Let me further tell you what prayer is like: In one of Grimm's stories there is a competition between a giant and a little tailor to see which is stronger. The giant throws a stone so high that it takes a very long time before it comes down again. The little tailor lets a bird fly, and it does not come down at all. Anything without wings always comes down again at the end. Prayer is the wing. You can surmount any giant hurdle through the wings of prayer. Attention is necessary for the end to be better obtained. It is necessary because without it something cannot obtain its full effect. The intention with which we set our heart on it must have merits. Prayer gives the requisite merit. It's written in (*DRA*, Matthew 6:5-6), "And when ye pray, you shall not be as the hypocrites, that love to stand and pray in the synagogues and corners of the streets, that they may be seen by men: Amen I say to you, they have received their reward. But you when you shall pray enter into your chamber, and having shut the door, pray to thy Father in secret: and your Father who sees in secret will repay you."

We are human. Our human mind is unable to remain aloof in prayer for long on account of the weakness of nature, because human weakness weighs down the soul to the level of inferior things. It happens quite often when the mind ascends to God by contemplation, next it wanders off through weakness. When you pray to God with psalms and hymns, let your mind attend to that which your lips pronounce. Set aside all the trappings where you seek your 'self' like on your smartphones. If you are so truly weakened by the distractions of the virtual world that you are unable to pray attentively, strive as much as you can to control yourself. Please make a note of the generosity of God He will pardon you, seeing that you are unable to stand in His presence in a becoming manner, not through negligence but through frailty. When praying, say little, pray as long as your attention is pure. Make the clamor in your heart register.

Faith is necessary in God to whom we pray. We need to believe that what we seek can only be achieved through Him. So humility is necessary on the part of the person praying, because he recognizes his neediness. Devotion is also necessary for what you're seeking. If your devotion is to excel in the game, you must be humble enough to attend to your desire. Because, remember neither prayer nor any other virtuous act, is meritorious without sanctifying grace. Grace is not a gift from God. It has to be rightly earned. It happens often and you listen to the murmur of your heart that God is not listening to you. Have you ever thought that you must have asked amiss, either inconsistently, or lightly? Prayer depends chiefly on faith. It depends chiefly on charity. It is through faith that man comes to know of God's presence and mercy.

The Greatest Teammate

Why has God established prayer? I think it's giving us some semblance of dignity when we sense defeat, when we recoil into our vulnerable self, when darkness covers our soul, to make us realize of the virtues to imbibe. It is written in The Bible, "great is your power and your wisdom is immeasurable." (*DRA,* Psalm 146:5).

Can we humbly accept that we're a little piece of Lord's creation? We must praise Him because He stirs our heart to take pleasure in praising Him that our heart takes strength in him. But who calls upon you Lord when he does not know you? What is the recourse for an ignorant person? Who will tell him that prayer is at the heart of a spiritual life? Prayer has the connotation of a 'Wish' and 'Aspiration' even if the person believes in the mystics of the land where he doesn't dwell. Prayer has a social reality in whatever time and space you live. Whether you pray in private or you pray in the communion of your place of worship. Can we dwell in isolation? Have we not survived for so long because we have lived as a community?

Pray! Pray and ask God to enable you to love you with all your strength with all your heart. 'From my God I shall be delivered from all temptation; and through my God I shall go over a wall' (*DRA*, Psalm 17: 30). Whatever you learn in your waking life, say your game, dedicate it to God first because when you excel you must avoid the vanities which have accompanied it. You haven't excelled in your life for any conceited purpose, right? You know every vain hope is empty where Lords' presence has not been felt. You also tremble with fear and at the same time burned with hope and exultation at Lord's mercy. "You have hated them that regard vanities, to no purpose. But I have hoped in the Lord: I will be glad and rejoice in your mercy. For you have regarded my humility, you have saved my soul out of distresses" (*DRA*, Psalm 30: 7–8).

The Greatest Teammate

Most importantly, it's the way of your being. How do you conduct your life by aligning yourself with Jesus? How do you respond to the Holy and through that you define your own relationship with yourselves? Don't you understand that it's such a dynamic relationship where your being desires for the fullness of life? You become the appreciator of life and beauty around you, don't you? If you have not then shifted the inclination of your heart, change the direction of the beast you're riding. You may rise rapidly; even sharper will be your fall. It's life. It's full of lapses. The only hope is in God's mercy when our heart becomes the repository of the mass culture and too many distractions. Empty your thoughts from all the frivolous voices and pray.

What prayer should you use? Who could be found to reconcile you to God? The true Mediator you showed to humanity in your secret mercy is Jesus. You sent Him so that from his example we should learn humility. He is 'the mediator between God and men, the man Christ Jesus' (*ESV*, 1 Timothy 2:5). St. Augustine writes in Confessions, "He appeared among us sinners as the immortal righteous one, mortal like humanity, righteous like God" (1998, P. 213). We make our prayer through our Lord Jesus Christ your Son, 'the man of your right hand, the Son of man whom you have strengthened' (*DRA*, Psalm 79: 18) to be a mediator between yourself and us.

You have made a practice of saying it through each morning with absolute attention. If during the recitation your attention wanders, you begin again until you have once succeeded in going through it with absolutely fervent attention. Sometimes you say the prayer out of sheer pleasure, but you only do it if you really feel the desire to recite it. There is silence, a silence which is not an absence of sound but which is the object of a positive sensation, more positive than that of sound.

As a mortal, you can access this silence. You may call it transcendence. It has the capacity to shine on the interior of your soul. It has beauty and order, which you can't define. It's indivisible. It's infinite. It's holy. It can never decrease or diminish. It exists independently of our prayer, eternally, quietly. Through prayer, you file your pure petition. Now tell me, can you prevent yourself from desiring?

In prayer, we don't manipulate God into the consciousness of our mind. It's the space in which we enter where everything dissolves, including time. The only end is God. The will moves our sense and reason towards the end. Therefore, nothing hinders the motion of our will, which desires its union with God. As soon as we reach a point of eternity in the soul, we have nothing more to do but to take care of it, for it will grow of itself like a seed. Then it is necessary to guard it, waiting in stillness, and to nourish it with the contemplation of prayers. Prayer shall lead you towards the authentic and pure values of life—truth, beauty and goodness—in whatever you pursue. Your sense of perception will become as sharp as that it can decipher the difference between the real and the illusory. The real becomes evident. We understand our time better. Our gaze remains fixed on what is visible. There shall be no attachment—neither to the failure, nor to the success.

It's written in (Luke 18:9-14) in the Parable of Pharisee about the prayer of the conceited who thinks of himself as self-righteous—Jesus told his disciple: "Two men went up to the temple to pray, one a Pharisee and the other a tax collector. "The Pharisee stood up and prayed about himself: 'God, I thank you that I am not like other people — robbers, evildoers, adulterers — or even like this tax collector. I fast twice a week and give a tenth of all I get.' "But the tax collector stood at a distance. He would not even look up to heaven, but beat his breast and said, 'God, have mercy on me, a sinner.'

I tell you that this man, rather than the other, went home justified before God. For all those who exalt themselves will be humbled, and those who humble themselves will be exalted."

The person who is praying ostentatiously is in fact satisfying his desire for a personal gain is not really discussed by Jesus. The real point is that seeing oneself in one's imagination, through the eyes of an imagined audience, is not good for a person to pray like the hypocrites do. However, praying in the way recommended by Jesus is always good, not because God will do something good because of the prayer, but because the act of genuine prayer is in itself good for the person who prays.

While all prayers are important, we should aim for the prayers appropriate to God's mercy and justice. It begins with the simple "Help!" of the crisis; it becomes the plaintive "What should I do?" of the dilemma; it emerges from the hindsight "What else could I have done?" It becomes confessional. Each of these is a prayer. Its purity is reached through time.

And what we find is a prayer, a prayer that articulates the call to God, and a prayer that at the same time embodies His response. His response is the presence of his Son, the empowerment of his Spirit, and the encouragement of his Word. Who could ask for anything more?

David L. Angeron

You can listen to the song by Mercy Me, "I Can only Image". Imagery in plain terms is understood in the context of the narrative of life, ministry, death, and the resurrection of Jesus. Image in this sense means that the divine nature of the Holy Trinity is the Image to whom man was made. Imitation of God does not signify subsequence, but only assimilation. It is written in (*DRA*, 1 Corinthians 11:7) "The man ought not to cover his head, for he is the image and the glory of God."

The Son alone is the image of the Father.

I can only imagine
What it will be like
When I walk by your side
I can only imagine
What my eyes would see
When your face is before me
I can only imagine
I can only imagine, yeah

Surrounded by your glory
What will my heart feel
Will I dance for you Jesus
Or in awe of You be still
Will I stand in your presence
To my knees will I fall
Will I sing hallelujah
Will I be able to speak at all
I can only imagine
I can only imagine (1999)

The Greatest Teammate

In sports, Imagery is visualization—the remarkable feature of the human mind is to experience the stimuli of the actual event, psychologically. For example, if you close your eyes, you should be able to imagine the sight and sound of your pitch entering the strike zone. Interestingly, this ability to use one's imagination is crucial to success in sport. Evidence suggests that mental imagery (visualization) is widely used by sport performers in an effort to enhance athletic performance. For example, the golfer Tiger Woods proclaimed the importance of imagery by stating that 'You have to see the shots and feel them through your hands' before addressing the ball (Pitt, 1998). Michael Phelps uses imagery to see and feel his strokes before a swimming race. He used simulation training. There's a story about him which is popular in the sports world that during the 200m of butterfly event of the 2008

Olympics, his goggles broke down for the last 100m of the race, which he won eventually. Apart from such anecdotal evidence, elite athletes (for example Golding, 1991) use mental imagery extensively while training for competition.

Imagery involves perception without sensation. If I ask you to close your eyes, can you visualize the color of your car, can you visualize the arcadia tree on your porch, and can you visualize the color of your attic wall. Yes, you can count the steps down to your attic. Can you go into the attic to fetch a candle after a massive blackout? Yes, you can. You can through some practice. Our waking life is full of sense-perception where visuals play an important part. Obviously, it occupies the most part of our brain. All we have to do is to use that part of the brain in stimulating all the visuals before our mind's eyes, minus the action. If we have to broadly define Mental Imagery, it's the multisensory construct that enables our mind to bring the absent object, and it's functionally equivalent to perception, in the sense that it shares the same brain machinery. It's the mental rehearsal of the key elements of the task. It's the contemplation of what might happen in the game. It's the subject of still going research that whether visualization enhances 'motor' or 'strength' tasks, but researchers have anecdotal evidence from elite athletes that they have used Mental Play before the game.

For what purposes do athletes use mental imagery? Athletes use imagery to engage in such activities as:

Learning and practicing sport skills (for example rehearsing swing mentally before going out to practice it on court)

Learning strategy (for example formulating a game plan before a match) emotions control (for example visualizing oneself behaving calmly in an anticipated stressful situation)

Learning to carry his game out confidently (for example 'seeing' oneself as confident and successful) focusing/refocusing (for example focusing on the 'feel' of a gymnastic routine)

Learning error correction (for example replaying a Pitch slowly in one's mind in order to rectify any flaws in it) improving interpersonal skills (for example imagining the best way to confront the coach about some issue)

Learning to manage pain (for example visualizing healing processes)

The athletes can also improve interpersonal skills by regulating their attitude on and off the field. They can manage their anxiety level. For some athletes, it's nerve wracking to approach their game. The athletes can course-correct their distractibility through mental imagery. They can wire their brain into focusing on key aspects of the game rather than frowning over the past mistakes.

Imagery is a way of perfecting yourself. You're made in the image of God. You imagine yourself and see your imperfections against the highest ideal, against a higher consciousness, and then you pray to Him and entreat for His help. Through prayer you raise your mind to a place which is infinite and limitless, and there you visualize and see the light.

Chapter 9
CONFIDENCE

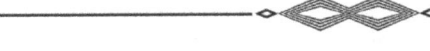

YOU CAN'T STOP ME BY ANDY MINEO

Why does a person lack confidence and become afraid to act? The reason is that he undermines his confidence by comparing himself with others. Both the lack of confidence and the paralyzing fear are linked with the absence of the thought about God. He is not a rebellious or disobedient person, but rather his mind is of one that doesn't think about his life in terms of God's will, God's grace, and God's love. So what is confidence?

In simple terms, confidence is the belief in yourself to enhance motivation at the time of need by aligning yourself with the will of God. Our ancestors used to go out and ignore the risk involved while foraging, combating, and exploring. Today, a fire fighter looks into the eye of raging fire while trying to douse it. Just look at the animals; they go about their operations at the break of sunlight. They do so again in the evening. That is the example of unbound confidence, even when they're unaware of it. Now, if you're an athlete, confidence works as a signaling move for your teammate—by seeing and believing in your capability they would rally around you and compete against an opponent no matter how formidable they are. It's the belief that makes you persevere in the pursuit of your goal, in spite of temptations that test your willpower. You persist by the grace of God.

Hence, confidence is a way to improve our self-image. It boosts our morale. Morale is helpful in taking difficult endeavors. For anyone, a poor self-image is painful to look at. We can safely say it is a fundamental human impulse to maintain self-esteem. We all want others to believe in our qualities. At the same time, it also works as a motivating factor. When we're working as a team, others put their beliefs in self-confident ones instead of self-doubting ones. There are pitfalls too, which we have to avoid. Sometimes we ignore vital information that is contrary to our belief. And it is a form of self-deception that could harm us and those who are involved. Over-confidence, or what I also call "fake confidence", stops us from assessing our ability correctly and we insist on going into the game even when we didn't perform well in practice.

We ignore the feedback because it would be detrimental to our self-esteem acknowledging it. It's a cognitive bias that we look at ourselves favorably and under weigh adverse signals. We go to any length to save our positive self—image and indulge in denial and self-justification.

So it's also important to look at ourselves critically and rationally. To always take a rosy picture of oneself is not positive thinking. It's true that athletes with high self-esteem don't need others validation. We should also remember that by consistently motivating ourselves into self-confidence would lead to high arousal, and that could make any athlete choke at a decisive moment. Have you ever given it a thought that why even ace players like Lionel Messi misses a penalty? Player like Tiger Woods misses a Putt. We would talk about choking later. Then under-confidence makes athletes choose performance-enhancing drugs to boost their self-esteem. What should we do then?

It's important to assess ourselves correctly that we're not setting over ambitious goals for ourselves. For that, it's important to understand ourselves better. Emotions run high in sports. Anger, fear, aggression, willful stalling, self-harm, there are so many things which govern our sporting life—confidence and self-belief would come when we pay attention to our 'self'.

Self can be broadly divided into following categories:
a) Spiritual Self
b) Material Self
c) Social Self
d) Ego Self

Let's define each category one by one and understand and how we can derive self-esteem and be confident by taking care of each "self" and how.

Spiritual self is the most enduring and intimate part of our being—an abstract way to deal with our consciousness. It's written in The Bible, "Such confidence we have through Christ before God. Not that we are competent in ourselves to claim anything for ourselves, but our competence comes from God" (*NIV,* 2 Corinthians 3:4-5). Our spiritual being is derived from the latent unity which is God. All we have to do is take care of our life, our thought through truth and integrity of our senses. There is one hope, one ground of confidence, one reliable promise—it is Christ's mercy.

As a mortal being our spirits derive hope in Christ's help because we're promised of help. The mind thus becomes assured of the undertaking it takes. It starts with confidence to accomplish the task at hand. The Bible says, "We want each of you to prove that you're working hard so that you will remain confident until the end. Then, instead of being lazy, you will imitate those who are receiving the promises through faith and patience" (*NIV,* Hebrew 6:11).

We take courage in holy confidence and accept whatever comes our way. An athlete's life is full of uncertainties, so we must develop the spirit of endurance and fortitude. The love of self in conformity with the will of Jesus would only bring satisfaction and success that is beyond the achievement and glories of the world. It starts with accepting life and helps us from the pitfalls of over-confidence at the time of immense success and raises us from the slump when we're under-confident by giving dignity to our failure. Confidence is the antidote to anxiety and fear. It gives us strength so we will not fall in the face of adversity. The courage doesn't come from foolish confidence in our own vain glory, where we put ourself in the danger of ignorance. We make false memory by not being attentive to our goals, which we have set out to achieve. The courage comes from the confidence of self-control. Yes, it's important to have some downtime after months of hard work in order to rejuvenate after a stupendous win, in order to self-assess during me-time. Confidence is to remain calm when passions run high. And it will only be developed through self-awareness and self-mastery.

As an Athlete, how do we accomplish self-awareness in order to gain confidence? It can be done through mental training. How? The first question that arises is what drives you. What do you want to achieve in the game? Do you have the desire to persist and accomplish something of importance? The skill involves dedicated planning, hard training, willingness to sacrifice instant gratification, and showing responsibility. By showing responsibility—you introspect your thoughts, feelings, and behaviors. You indulge in the honest appraisal of your progress so far. Self-evaluation is an important maker of a confident athlete. This is the mental side of the game.

A confident athlete believes in productive thinking. It is the ability to manage thoughts and emotion in face of changing events for his or her well-being. The task of problem solving takes priority even during the match. A successful athlete changes his strategy when an error is made. They adapt according to the situation. And it works as a motivating factor for him and his team as well.

Self-confidence comes from the athlete's ability to turn setbacks into an opportunity. It's the signifier of his capability and talent. It's the sign of his resilience and unshakable belief to achieve success. A highly skilled athlete drives his confidence from his performance, from his technical expertise in the game. He is perceptual and decides accordingly. He can anticipate the game and turn the tide in his favor. His attention is sharp and with his sustained focus can win any game. He can manage his energy strategically by not showing his anger, arousal, excitement, and fear. The competitive sport elicits a high range of intense emotions because of the value and rewards attached to it. A confident athlete manages it effectively and knows the optimal level of energy needed for the game. He knows how to push the boundary of emotional and physical pain. In a high-pressure game, he can assess his nervousness naturally instead of being hard on himself.

Through sustained mental training, an athlete comes to a point where he has the clear sense of his identity like "who am I?" that allows him to take care of his psychological well-being and self-worth. He will not fall into the trap of conformity.

Team confidence builds on the integrity, and faith of the athlete defined above. It will have the confidence of collective resources and abilities to win a game. Confidence brings cohesion, which is the ability of the team sticking together in the pursuit of its goals. Confidence opens the channel of communication within the team where information flows and opens the channel of blocked imagination when the team is David who is fighting the Goliath. Confidence is instilled by a leader who takes charge of the team and signals his heroics on the field as motivation for the rest of the team.

Self-assessment also involves when the athlete understands his bias, prejudice, and also understands the subculture of the sports he plays. A sporting world is an insular world where mental training is not considered 'macho' where it could get stigmatized. He understands what negative body image is, what hazing and violence could bring. He understands things external to him that his self is made of 'I'. He creates this 'I' by destroying it until he understands that the value in him comes from Jesus. It has been given to him as a stream that springs forth from his consciousness—it must be renewed by being a humble petitioner. The spiritual self is achieved when he saves the 'I' in him from external affliction. Only then the purity of 'I' is achieved.

Confidence builds inside of you when you take care of your mental side by focusing on:

a) Productive Thinking (Manage emotions well)

b) Task (Specific and achievement based)

c) Performance (Skill based, which is Tactical/Strategic)

d) Identity (Spiritual)

Now come to the material self—the material self starts with the body which is in each of us, then it extends itself to clothes, then to our relationships like how it's with our parents, siblings, and partners, to the things that we possess. When a relationship dies, a part of us dies. How healthy your attachment is with people and things around you, is an important determinant of driving your confidence. If they're insulted, then we're insulted. If they do something wrong, then we feel embarrassed. Our home comes next, which is the repository of our intimate memories. The spaces of your bedroom room are full of vacant emotions or love—drive your emotional well-being. How confidently will you perform on the field depends on this? There are certain things we want to own in our lives—it's the fruit of our labor, like a signed glove from your hero that you possess—that he signed in an admiration of a rising talent. Now you have forgotten that at an opponent's field. Would you feel devastated or not while sitting behind home plate and catching pitches in the next game? We're assimilated into everything that we love, appreciate, and respect.

Let's start with body: As an athlete, it's absolutely imperative to take care of our body self-esteem. It's an important construct that drives our self-worth, beliefs, characteristics, and cognition to evaluate our actions. Your sports competence is based on your physical condition. Maintain certain weights during your sporting life. There are some sports where you have to maintain your upper body strength. If it's good, you have naturally taken care of your confidence in the physical strength of your body. You try to keep it stable. Even then you self-evaluate yourself negatively when you lose some of your strength before completing your 10-mile run. Exercise is important to maintain your self-esteem according to Rosenberg Scale—which is not completely true if we cultivate our physical well-being by only keeping this aspect in mind. It's a valuable marker for evaluating ourselves and coming to a conclusion where we lack or how we have progressed. Like, you're recuperating from an injury and have gained weight over the time. Your confidence will increase as you progress with favorable result.

Family: They give emotional security and much needed cushion in the face of an adverse situation. Emotions can affect individual performance. Some athletes are so emotional that they take time to recuperate from a loss. Some athletes are impassive, and they rarely show emotion. Fear and anxiety are the part and parcel of the game.

So persistence and engagement are important while you're in the game. You don't want to go blank in an important match. Emotional responses might play havoc with your physiological, motor, and cognitive functioning. High emotional response sometimes overwhelms cognitive functioning. That is why we hear athletes lashing out at the opponent, or the referee, and even on fans. Hence positive emotions are important in felicitating performance in difficult condition by regulating physiological and cognitive functioning. Happiness and joy fuel your engagement in the game. Family is a great source of positive emotions. At the start of the chapter we talked about choking. We must understand what it is and how do we manage it.

It's a great killer of confidence. Jana Novotna is a professional Tennis Player who has Wimbledon, Olympic Medals to her credits, visibly choked during a ladies singles final match of Wimbledon in 1993 against Steffi Graf. She just began to lose her emotional control over the game. Choking happens when pressure mounts and excessive anxiety just depletes the athlete's performance. The harder they try, the worse the situation becomes. Often, an increased drive alleviates the performance, but in the case of choking it actually debilitates the athlete. The attention of the athlete completely shifts away from the game. The distraction happens because the athlete is more focused on the situation after the game that what would happen if he lost the match. Sometimes the athletes are too focused on enhancing his skills and that results in heighten self-consciousness. He starts with a mentality that he can't afford to lose the match. He motivates himself so much that it works as counterproductive. We talked about over-confidence at the start of the chapter. The pressure mounts so much that they try to take control of the skills innate to them. Anxious athletes in order to maintain their level of performance put an extra effort into their game which might give them an immediate pay-off, but as the game progresses, they lose the drive to go on in the game.

It's important to adapt a right approach towards the game in order to gain confidence and we have already discussed the spiritual and Material well-being of the self. Next is the social self.

Social self is the recognition we receive from our peers. We're social animal and are naturally inclined to see ourselves favorably noticed. We all crave for recognition. Athletes don't perform in isolation. They're very much part of the public life. Your face on a billboard at Times Square would surely not make or break your game, but it will surely build a positive image. So many people carrying a distinct image of yours in their mind when they see you in an advertisement before a Super bowl game.

Opinion matters, and it affects us in different ways. So, we constantly work towards the emotional flow of our being. "For the Lord will be your confidence and will keep your feet from being caught" (*ESV*, Proverb 3:26). Spiritual well-being should be the basis of your life. Just take care of it and you can rest easy. It will bring balance to your life.

Ego self is not far from your spiritual self. Spiritual self is the pure ego. But life is in transition, temporally and spatially. And there are so many distractions and influences. The living world has so much to offer.

Money and fame have its own way to play with our mind. Vanity is one of them. Our ego self is defined by the means through which we have defined our lives. How this subjective life of ours is distinguished from others? Can up say for sure that the unity of your consciousness is with the God? If yes, then you're on the right path.

As we have seen, confidence is a state of mind where self-belief comes from numerous factors. We need to take care of those factors as an athlete. We shall discuss more that are minor but important factors.

a) Self-Acceptance: It is a form of positive attitude towards ourselves—being able to evaluate the good and bad aspects of our qualities rationally. It is the start of realization and identifying one's true potential. It starts with bodily acceptance. In sports, it's important that the athletes value themselves and perceive themselves as competent. Now acceptance of the self comes from how as an athlete our performance has been perceived by our loved ones and our coach. Their opinion matters. We adapt accordingly during our game. It's likely that we perform better than before, and there is an increase in confidence. On the other hand, some athletes accept themselves unconditionally. They set high standard for themselves, which act as counter-productive when they're unable to achieve those targets. They don't depend on the approval of others.

b) Self-Compassion: It is the athletes' desire to heal himself or herself with kindness rather than berate himself with harsh criticism. It's useful in the time of pain and failure. The compassion comes from the fact that the individual's body has certain limitations. The compassion towards oneself brings us to self-conscious emotions that we need to understand, like shame, guilt, pride, and embarrassment. Here an individual interacts with a collective bunch of people like his teammates and evaluate himself by reflecting upon success, failure, and the subculture of the sport he plays. These emotions are strong and have the capability of regulating an athlete's life. It could act as an essential motivator of an athlete's feeling and behavior. We only talk about basic emotions, like happiness, sadness, anger, fear, and joy, but it's also important to talk about guilt and shame. Self-conscious emotions come from the evaluation of behavior through social yardstick. Approval and disapproval come through social acceptance. These emotions also don't have any visible facial representation or gestures, so it's hard to detect.

Even a coach wouldn't be aware of the fact that his player is carrying the guilt of missing a goal. The reason is only known to him that he has transgressed the line and broken the night curfew by binge partying before a crucial game. Shame is a painful emotion. It comes from humiliation when an athlete fails to meet his or her own standard, then a cycle of chronic self-blame starts. It could lead to depression, anxiety, and negative self-image. Embarrassment is a negative emotion where an athlete fails to maintain his public self. Any event like sudden prejudice or racial rant on a public platform has the capacity to break an athlete's career. Pride is a positive emotion where an athlete values himself and constructs his behavior around it. It shouldn't be excessive pride where the 'self' takes a grand proportion, and we think of ourselves as superior in others. The real pride comes from respecting one's effort after the completion of specific goals. Excessive pride is powerful and may bring positive achievements to the athlete because it's solely focused on the self-attainment of the goal. But such athletes are unable to maintain their success in the long run because they're only focused on themselves. Narcissism, self-aggrandizement wouldn't take you anywhere, being social and conscientious certainly would. Self-compassion is important to bring back lost confidence in oneself.

Sport is a place where athletes from different race and culture come together as a team, as an opponent. So, compassion is important in establishing the culture of belief in the game. The game should win.

c) Self-Doubt: Even after taking care of how positively we look at our game, whether our goal is achievement based or how task-specific and tactical our approach is towards the game, doubt creeps in the back of our mind. Suddenly, we become uncertain of our abilities. Self-doubt can be disarming because we concoct several situations in our mind before the game starts that we didn't practice under a better coach, that the opponent is formidable, and that the management spends frugally on the team. If later we fail, we attribute the same reasons that we invented before the game to the failure. Or Self-doubt can also lead to over achievement. The moment doubt takes its roots, we strike it down with reinforced vigor and that would lead to enhancement of capabilities in order to save our self from impending failure. Experts say a moderate self-doubt is actually beneficial because it stops an athlete from being complacent and over-confidant.

Yes, the relationship between self-confidence and performance is much more complex than we have thought. We have discussed the important attributes of a confident self. And that brings us to the last point of self-awareness.

d) Self-Awareness: It's the knowledge of 'I' and 'Me' where 'I' is the subject of different stimulus and experience and 'Me' is the object and receiver of information, which 'I' have experienced. The 'Me' self is attentive and uses the information for self-recognition and self-identification. High level of self-awareness leads to correct evaluation of one's performance and adapt accordingly. The athletes know themselves better. In a high-pressure game, they zone themselves out from the extra noise and narrow down their attention to the game. Sometimes media circus around a personal relationship of an athlete can work as a distraction because it brings too much attention on him, so it's important to reduce a high level of self-awareness to low level of self-awareness. Sometimes elite athletes find themselves in fan frenzy before an important game because of the standard they have set for themselves. The situation demands an escape. If the athlete is fully prepared and won't find any deficiency in the self, he sees through the pressure. If the athlete is not fully prepared and under-confident that he couldn't deliver this time, he tried to fulfill this lack in the self with binge eating or alcoholism. There comes a time when an athlete manipulates self-awareness through distractions like watching Rocky Balboa movie series if he's into boxing or listen to the song such as this by Andy Mineo's 'You Can't Stop Me' which has beautiful lyrics that goes like:

They try to shut us down, and it ain't gon' slide
Only thing I fear is God and he on my side
That's the confidence of God, cause he got me
That's why I really feel like
You can't stop me
That's all you got? Come on with it
That's all you got?

You can't stop me
(You) don't got the power, (can't) shut me down
(Stop), that's not an option, (me) I'm my biggest problem
(You) don't got the power, (can't) shut me down
, that's not an option
You can't stop me (2014).

The athlete also thus indulges in self-talk to boost his self-confidence. Self-talk connects the two parts of the self: The 'I' and 'Me' into one thread of consciousness.

It is written in the Bible, "Therefore do not throw away your confidence, which has a great reward. For you have need of endurance, so that when you have done the will of God you may receive what is promised" (*ESV, Hebrew 10:35-36*).

The Greatest Teammate

Chapter 10
The Greatest Teammate

"Awesome God" by R-Swift

CHAPTER 10: THE GREATEST TEAMMATE

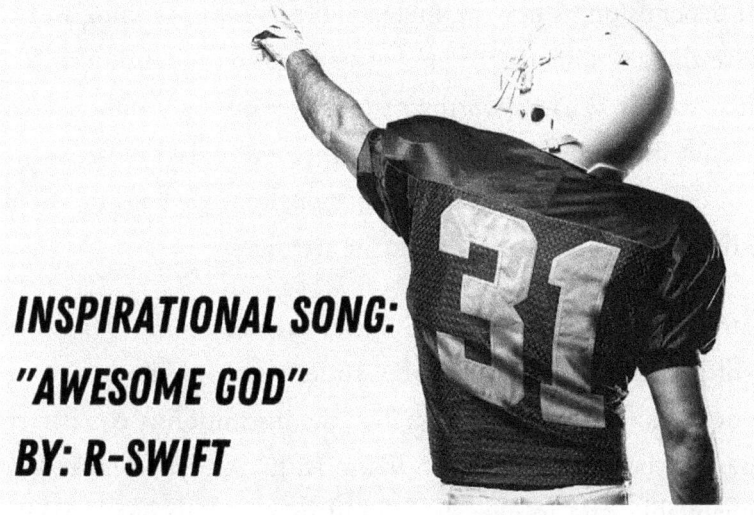

INSPIRATIONAL SONG:
"AWESOME GOD"
BY: R-SWIFT

A teammate is an enabler. He interacts with you on a visual and auditory level. He gives you a sign when you're in the field enduring the attack of your opponent. You act accordingly. Later you pay your gratitude and enjoy time together with your

The Greatest Teammate

teammates. These are the teammates who exist beside you. There's one teammate who is divine and lives inside you. You exist because you carry his attributes.

For God to present Himself in us, He doesn't need special things to be produced in us. Our body and life are proof enough of His presence in us. We unite ourselves with God; it's our way of loving Him. We are united with God because we depend immediately on Him. This is how God becomes our greatest teammate.

God does good things for you all the time. God has sustained you so far and will continue to do so in the future. He encourages you to trust Him. God will take care of your anxiety and fear. God knows about your fundamental needs. Still, we remain anxious about our future. It depends on us how we imagine our lives by ascribing worth to what we think is essential. What is worthy of our attention in our fragmented world? What is worthy of our blood, sweat, and energies when the culture of consumerism is redefined every day? What is the purpose of our lives when fantasy and illusion are woven around us as the tapestry of truth? Who am I? Who are we then?

According to Aristotle, we are social creatures. The goal and purpose of our lives are shaped by the stories we share, the stories we imagine by giving wings to our thoughts, the institutions we make, to make our lives bearable and worth living with dignity, to make our places inhabitable, and to give shapes and meanings to our lives. By coming together, we bring glory and grace of God to our doorsteps. We bring wholeness, healing, and reconciliation with the world by animating the spirit of God. God is our greatest teammate. We're united by his will. We can endeavor to self-making by sharing God's goods. We can flourish together. It's such a humbling experience that we're profoundly dependent on God and others. Yes, we're a team.

It's written in the Bible, "Therefore I tell you, do not worry about your life, what you will eat or drink; or about your body, what you will wear. Is not life more than food, and the body more than clothes? Look at the birds of the air; they do not sow or reap or store away in barns, and yet your heavenly Father feeds them. Are you not much more valuable than they? Can any of you by worrying add a single hour to your life (*NIV,* Matthew 6:25-27)?

What is a team if we try to understand through sports? A team is a group of people who interact together and influence each other to achieve a common goal. By doing so, they shape each other's psychological and social identities. What are the important attributes of a team?

a) Cohesiveness
b) Interaction
c) Goals
d) Identity
e) Structure

Our task becomes easy when we're already living and practicing our lives through the essence of God. By the very virtue of interdependence at the community level, we instill the value of cohesiveness in us. The structure could be our sports team, family, or society. Our goal is aligned with God. This is possible only when there is interaction and flow of information. We imagine and shape our identities through these interactions. After fulfilling the above criteria, the task is divided into the minutest details according to the quality of contribution by the members of the team.

A cohesive team is where the members influence and motivate each other into self-awareness—where one can only improve and excel in their given task. The constant evaluation can lead to stress and anxiety when the task is difficult. Then your team is the microcosm of a social structure that would arouse a feeling of security and belonging. This sense of security will keep your mind at ease. Individual performance will increase naturally when value is added to the team through the efforts of each member of the team—when the value is transferred to each individual in return.

Team success can lead to stability and collective efficacy, performance, and success through synergy. Individual success can lead to self-esteem, trust, reduced anxiety, clear goals for the future, and above all self-acceptance. Sports like baseball depend on individual performance and team cohesion. So, for any successful team, we must have a clearly defined goal, a sense of purpose, team and individual accountability, cohesiveness, honest communication, and trust. It's how a team takes care of their collective behavior in check. The team is better placed to assess the cause of their success and failure—whether it exists inside of the team or outside of the team. The team is better placed to check their stability over some time.

A player would respond emotionally and with the best of their capabilities, with a sound mind, to any challenge. The pride and self-esteem of the team would be high. The factors that are outside of his control like luck and refereeing shall not bother him forever. But, such is life. Some pitfalls bother us like a team losing a big game at the last second. It can lose its bearings because the collective shame of failure would be high. At this point, God will take care of your emotional needs. You will show courage by facing the reality at hand. When you bring God as your teammate, courage will be one of your main attributes. What is courage?

Courage gives you good hope. It's in the Bible, "Jesus looked at them and said, "With man, this is impossible, but not with God; all things are possible with God" (Mark 10:27). You can bear and endure any frightening situation to the best of your reason. In a sporting life, pain is inevitable, whether it's physical or psychological. You must acknowledge it, but you can't afford to be reckless. You can't be insensitive to what the reason commands. You have torn your ligament or a tendon and without nursing it back to health you impetuously come back to the field—this recklessness would take you in for a long haul. This is not courage.

On the other hand, a team of low spirit could exceed any fear. For example, if they're facing a team that is technically far superior, they end up crippling themselves physically and mentally before the match starts. You're going into the game with a faint hope that some miracle would happen and save the team from an embarrassing defeat. Courage is a means of acting with dignity. Courage endows you with a defiant spirit. The Lord says in (*ESV,* Joshua 1:9), "Have I not commanded you? Be strong and courageous. Do not be frightened, and do not be dismayed, for the LORD your God is with you wherever you go."

Ignorant are those who don't believe the words of God. They have no claim to merit. For team building, we need a state of mind that is open to the intelligence of God that is open to true knowledge. After that, come the interpersonal relations and goal settings. Only then the information would flow smoothly among the team members when there is no room for individual conceit and vanity. The individuals would come together and help each other by being goal-specific and distribute the pressure by focusing on action-oriented tasks. Even when off the track two athletes of a team can take the cohesiveness of the team by coming together in the Gym or while they decide to clock 10 miles in the morning. Only then your strength coach would come along in building your character along with your physical and mental strength.

By building this kind of environment in the Team, an individual would shine forth with his distinctive ability. He would find a place suitable for him in the team structure and act as an active agent. The other point that comes out while we're discussing team building is team communication.

TEAM COMMUNICATION is how two people interact in a group with thoughts and feelings, how information and knowledge are exchanged through verbal and non-verbal messages. A team leader and a coach can easily identify the spirit of the team through body postures and how a player positions his body. For verbal communication, the hallmark of a cohesive team is the unambiguous, precise, and clear exchange of information. And yet the exchange is so discrete that if an opposition team is training in the same field or playing during the competition would not identify what just has been exchanged.

Many sports involve players exchanging their positions consistently. Sports like basketball, football are prime examples. Players covertly and overtly communicate during the game all the time when they're taking a corner shot or when they communicate through the magic of a play action pass. Research findings also show that the tendency to receive messages visually makes the players better at receiving the auditory message. The players' traits also improve when they become more expressive. Their self-esteem improves when they positively and self-consciously communicate with their team. Furthermore, if players indulge in a fluid exchange of information and are mentally accommodating, their anxiety level reduces to a manageable level. In the end, we have a healthy team.

A healthy team leads to positive relations amongst its team members. The positive relation, in return, leads to better attendance, punctuality, and overall discipline. Players don't drop out when their self-esteem tanks due to bad performance or when their relationship fails. Cognitive outcomes like personal satisfaction with their growth are reported to be on a higher level. Now add God to that healthy team and they would be as calm as sea amid a raging storm. Like Jesus rebuked the wind, "That day when evening came, he said to his disciples, "Let us go over to the other side." Leaving the crowd behind, they took him along, just as he was, in the boat. There were also other boats with him. A furious squall came up, and the waves broke over the boat so that it was nearly swamped. Jesus was in the stern, sleeping on a cushion. The disciples woke him and said to him, "Teacher, don't you care if we drown?" He got up, rebuked the wind, and said to the waves, "Quiet! Be still!" Then the wind died down, and it was completely calm. He said to his disciples, "Why are you so afraid? Do you still have no faith" (Mark 4:35-40)?

When you take God as your teammates, you add value and worth to your endeavor. You add attributes that would help you grow as an athlete. We have already discussed courage. What are the other attributes that you could develop by just keeping the essence of God alive in your heart?

The greatness of the Soul lies in its acts—acts that are virtuous according to their worth. You would be foolish to act contrary to your claim of your greatness. You would be vain if you brag about your greatness when you have nothing to show. In today's time, worth is assigned to the material goods that we add to self-validate our existence in society. We forget easily the greatest worth we should assign to and aiming to acquire is God's will. That is the noblest of things. A great soul is concerned with his honor and dishonor in the task he takes. He acts accordingly. He will not be overjoyed by good fortune or aggrieved by bad fortune. He wouldn't turn over-proud or arrogant after setting the record in clocking the highest home run in a season. A great soul knows how and when to sacrifice for the larger good.

He is always eager to serve his team, his community, the best possible way he could. He speaks freely because his thoughts are not chained with contempt for others. He heaps praise because he's not envious of his teammate's achievements. He never speaks ill of anybody because he holds no grudge, but he knows how to answer those who act insolently. He will shine when no one does because he has willed his desire with God's desire. His wisdom lies in believing in the words of God that he says in the Bible, "No temptation has overtaken you that is not common to man. God is faithful, and he will not let you be tempted beyond your ability, but with the temptation, he will also provide the way of escape, that you may be able to endure it" (*ESV*, 1 Corinthians 10:13).

Gentleness is the means to manage our anger. He remains calm in difficult situations and never acts according to his passion. He applies reason and rationality to the situation before acting. A gentleman might fail by believing in forgiveness, but by doing so he might attract ridicule because forgiveness is a foolish act in some eyes. Because people don't know about the value God has ascribed to the act of forgiveness, It's written in the Bible, "And whenever you stand praying, forgive, if you have anything against anyone, so that your Father also who is in heaven may forgive you your trespasses" (*ESV,* Mark 11:25).

It doesn't mean a man who is gentle lacks perception and is not mindful of the pain. He is. He knows what is bad has a small shelf life. It destroys itself by its nature. A bad thing can't sustain itself like a lie.

A coach has a heck of a time dealing with a person who flies off the handle at the slightest provocation. Team members have a tough time dealing with a person who holds bitterness for a long time. It's hard to reconcile with them. An angry athlete believes in revenge and that might make him perform better and he may win matches for his team, but it will not be a desirable win because the athlete acted on his own.

Magnificence is the virtue of a person who owes gratitude to God (gratitude flows to the one who gives) for his privileged position in society and then gives back to society with good intent. He is not ostentatious with his display. He shares what he has for what is noble and just. Jesus feeds the four thousand by being magnificent with his compassion. During those days another large crowd gathered. Since they had nothing to eat, Jesus called his disciples to him and said, "I have compassion for these people; they have already been with me three days and have nothing to eat. If I send them home hungry, they will collapse on the way, because some of them have come to a long distance." His disciples answered, "But where in this remote place can anyone get enough bread to feed them?" "How many loaves do you have?" Jesus asked. "Seven," they replied (Mark 8:2-5).

Truthfulness is praiseworthy. He acknowledges his qualities to God first and never boasts about his skills in the first place. He is not a pretender. His speech and action speak of the truth he possesses.

He guards himself against the falsity in whatever situation he is in. His reputation is not goal-oriented or money-oriented or for the sake of any gains. He acts like his character demands him to. Someone who has given to falsehood enjoys it in itself or longs for benefits he's not capable of. A truthful athlete knows himself better. He knows that it's written in the Bible that, "The plans of the heart belong to man, but the answer of the tongue is from the LORD. All the ways of a man are pure in his own eyes, but the LORD weighs the spirit. Commit your work to the LORD, and your plans will be established" (*ESV,* Proverb 16:1-3).

Ambition is ascribing worth to what a person longs for and harbors the feeling for the same in his heart for some time. Like desire, it is external to him and very likely he has no control over it. He is over-ambitious if he longs for honor far exceeding his worth. And he is under ambitious who doesn't feel honored about the noble thing he does. For it is written in the Bible, "For all that is in the world—the desires of the flesh and the desires of the eyes and pride in possessions—is not from the Father but is from the world" (*ESV,* 1 John 2:16).

You are good because his mercy is forever. St. Augustine rightly says that by his grace the darkness has been enlightened and the weakness has been swallowed up by the strength. Everything that comes out as the word of God is eternal. It has no end. It's not like one thing is said after another in succession leading to a definitive conclusion. It has the simultaneity of eternity. Since we know this truth and can't be ungrateful. We accept things humbly and seek pleasure accordingly. What pleasure means in this context?

The Greatest Teammate

Pleasure is the center of the value-seeking process of human lives. We avoid pain. It clubs us with the question we raised at the start of this chapter that our lives are governed by ascribing worth to things that exist outside of us. We drive the meaning of our lives from it. We're into sports, so game brings a certain joy into our lives. When we win, it becomes a pleasurable event for our family. So the family is important. God is important because we find strength in him. Our teammates are important because of their collective effort. We must answer before we go seeking pleasure that at what cost and to what end. If pleasure is good quality, then it must conclude at some point. The human good is always limited.

It's only God's good that is immortal and unlimited. Pleasure should work as a restoration or replenishment to our being against the trials and tribulations of our lives so that we could function properly. If you're still unsure of what you should pursue, then listen to the wisdom of what the good Lord has to say in the Bible.

As Jesus started on his way, a man ran up to him and fell on his knees before him. "Good teacher," he asked, "What must I do to inherit eternal life" "Why do you call me good?" Jesus answered. "No one is good—except God alone. You know the commandments: You shall not murder, you shall not commit adultery, you shall not steal, you shall not give false testimony, you shall not defraud, honor your father and mother." "Teacher," he declared, "all these I have kept since I was a boy." Jesus looked at him and loved him. "One thing you lack," he said. "Go, sell everything you have, and give to the poor. At this, the man's face fell. He went away sad because he had great wealth (Mark 10:17-22).

We fret about the future, which is always receding into the past. One day the sound ceases and the future becomes the past. How does this future that does not yet exist diminish? For the mind desires an expectation from the future. The past exists. Who can deny that? It exists as memories in our minds. We can't extend the present time because it passes in a flash. So what is continuous along the continuum? Attention is continuous. It is through the attention we observe what is future will be absent when it presents itself. So the expectation of the future is a futile act. That is why Simone Weil speaks that attention is the rarest form of generosity. It is the orientation of all the attention that the soul directs towards God. The highest part of the attention is when you relate yourself to the act of God.

Jesus is the way that leads us to God. The cross exhibits all the virtues. St Augustine says, "As whosoever wishes to live perfectly can do nothing other than to disdain what Christ on the Cross disdains and desire what Christ desires. If you want to find the example of charity, then we must bring to our mind what has been said in (*NIV,* John 15:13) "Greater love has no one than this: To lay down one's life for one's friends." Jesus died on the cross. If you're looking for the example of patience, the most perfect is found on the cross. If you're looking for the example of humility, look to the crucified one. If you're looking for an example of obedience, follow him who was made obedient even in death… If you're looking for an example of contempt for worldly things, follow the one who is King of Kings and Lord of Lords and who possesses treasures of wisdom, but who despite all that was stripped bare, mocked, whipped, crowned with thorns, given gall and sour wine to drink, and put to death on the Cross.

The Greatest Teammate

An act of forgiveness is not seen as manly today, but Jesus explicitly asks us, "Truly I tell you, if anyone says to this mountain, 'Go, throw yourself into the sea,' and does not doubt in their heart but believes that what they say will happen, it will be done for them. Therefore, I tell you, whatever you ask for in prayer, believe that you have received it, and it will be yours. And when you stand praying, if you hold anything against anyone, forgive them, so that your Father in heaven may forgive you your sins" (Mark 11:23-25).

R Swift brings the same wisdom through his song, "Awesome God". You should listen to this song and may relate to the virtues that we have just discussed above:

Our God is an awesome God
He reigns from heaven above
With wisdom power and love
Our God is an awesome God

All power he contains it, the man on his own
Abandoned the throne to approach the cross stainless
Death couldn't shake him or derail
Three nails could pierce but couldn't break him
or make him appear taken
Away from his mere nature (2009).

What is happiness—if we ponder it for a second, then we would of course align our desire with Jesus' desire? That is how the divine presents itself in our being. Now this divine is far superior, and it points to a fact that we can be united with God by the intellect. If we could honor His presence by performing our task the best way we could, because excellent things don't come in bulk, would be our way to arrive at happiness. It's written in the Bible the answers you seek to questions like where do you want to go, which way do you want to go, Jesus answered, "I am the way and the truth and the life. No one comes to the Father except through me."

Happiness is contemplative when fulfilling our task after tending to the immediate necessities of life. When we become self-sufficient, we justly extend the goods bestowed upon us by God to others.

The Greatest Teammate

Chapter 11
Good Life: Losing Everything & Found Everything

"Good Life" by Audio Adrenaline

The Greatest Teammate

All of man's energy goes into striving for what is good for his or her life.

Sometimes he gropes in the dark, sometimes he shines on the journey he has taken. A small mistake can set him back swiftly from his goal before he could know it. So, he assesses his movements and his ambition regularly. He is clear about what he seeks to gain. Is he? Because, when he leaves many miles behind and finds that the path was deceptive. It's a well-trodden path. But, it was not good for him. He believed in the common wisdom and now he has to restart.

The reason he believes in the collective rationale of the certain goal is that he finds so many alongside him. They heap praise on him because of the ego herd needs. Everyone validates each other's positions in society. What is wrong with that? The only thing wrong with this and it's a profound point that he ends up being an imitation. It's a recipe for disaster. If wrongs start piling up, and mind you there're so many committing it, society would collapse. One goes astray and becomes an instigator for others, leading everyone astray. Is that a good life? Is that a life worth pursuing? A life where you trust other's judgments?

Did you trust the man because he wears good clothes? What are you going to gain from it by deciding your course of life by looking at the color and shine on the other man's body? It fails your mind when you'll ponder over it. On the other hand, you can't seek the knowledge of life on your own. You will need a guide. How can you identify him with whom you can trust? Of course, He is a knower of everything and is of superior intellect. "My son, do not forget my teaching, but keep my commands in your heart, for they will prolong your life many years and bring you peace and prosperity" (*NIV*, Proverb 3:1-2).

When you're not an island and exist alone in isolation, you get influenced. You get inspired. We all have some examples and models that we follow. How can you identify him—a man same as you made of bone and flesh? You have one light, a trustworthy and reliable light by which you can identify between a pretender and a solemn person, a hypocrite and a real person, between truth and falsehood, and that light is your soul. Let your soul's goodness guide you in identifying another soul of purity. Let us seek that is not merely good in its outward appearance, but is beautiful and balanced from the inside.

We don't need to go far away seeking it—it is situated near to us; so that we can reach it by just stretching our hands. An athlete is even more limited. His stadium and his grounds are the core of his existence. Next is his home. If we ask him to find truth in a secluded place tucked some thousand miles away from his home—man, that would be unfair.

A good life is in harmony with its nature. You will need two things to find that homeostasis in your life: First, you will need a mind that is rational and sound that is vigorous and brave that can endure life's hardships. A mind that is attentive to the needs of the body, a mind that can adapt to new situations, a mind that doesn't become anxious at the slightest change of weather, a mind that shines when the fortunes shine by not becoming its slave, a benevolent mind that is not cruel. A good life is to have a mind that is independent and resolute. A mind that desires honor as the only good and everything else as mere addition and subtraction that doesn't decrease the highest good. What the highest good? The highest good is beyond death. The highest good that is eternal that never alters is perfect. That is the second thing we need to be attentive to—living our lives following God's discipline. It's the most beautiful of riches of all, more than all the riches of the world.

It's written in the Bible, "Long life is in her right hand; in her left hand are riches and honor. Her ways are pleasant ways, and all her paths are peace. She is a tree of life to those who take hold of her; those who hold her fast will be blessed" (*NIV*, Proverb 3: 16-18).

A man with the right disposition as described above will inevitably find his life easy to deal with. His life will be good. His happiness will be profound. His life is good because he never cared about his fortune. He doesn't seek goodness that is external to him. But his knowledge of life is driven from the goodness which is his own. It doesn't mean he is free from desire and fear that is why he is happy. Any inanimate object is without fear and desire. We can say more or less about animals. Can we say that the chair in our dining hall looks very happy? Of course not, a chair has any understanding of happiness, what is good, and what is desirable. A man is no less than an animal or a chair—if he doesn't have a rational mind; whose reason is warped to appoint that he is detrimental to himself, and who is far away from the truth by not believing in the wisdom of Lord.

Only a man of reason can learn from his past, he will not gloat about his anticipated fortune. He will not lay supine in the present. Therefore, a good life consists of sound judgment. The Lord asks us in (*NIV*, Proverb 3: 21-23), "My son don't let wisdom and understanding out of your sight, preserve sound judgment and discretion; they will be life for you, an ornament to grace your neck. Then you will go on your way in safety, and your foot will not stumble." A good life is satisfied with its present situation. Good life shows contentment when it has the world at its feet, a good life endures; a good life values its existence because the divine dwells in it. A good life knows pleasure is fickle. It extinguishes the moment it gives delight. It holds a very small place in a good life. A good life takes happiness and pleasure as the byproduct of its fortune. The highest good is harmonizing life's spirit with the essence of God.

You will find freedom, beauty, and harmony of life in it. So come and let the virtue guide your life, let it set the life's standard for you. It will bring moderation when you lose self-control after achieving remarkable things in your life. It will keep you in check when you become overly ambitious. A virtuous life doesn't seek commoditization of itself. True happiness resides in virtue. You will not consider anything in life whether good or bad weighing on the fact that it has been followed by keeping god's good in mind.

Again, what is a good life? Is the good the only purpose to follow in your life? If this is the kind of life we want to live, then we must know what that good is. If not, then there's no point in discussing life because it has fallen into an illusion, a life without a purpose is a life filled with false hope. We all work towards an end. The world would call us deranged if we float aimlessly in the world. Aristotle defined the end as "that for the sake of which a thing is done, and the good as that at which all things aim." Why do you seek something when you know it will bring trouble? A psychotropic substance can give you an adrenaline jump, but it can also disqualify you before the big event you have been waiting for.

The Greatest Teammate

How can human conduct go wrong when we're seeking goodness all along? Everything that exists is good in itself because he's contributing in some way to the harmony of the world. He has some perfection, which is good for something. It doesn't mean that a being is good for everything. So there are various degrees of goodness. We don't follow the good for its own sake but as a means to further good, especially to achieve the highest good. It is desirable only because it leads to something more desirable. Let's take the example of necessary good, like you have to learn the skill to survive to get back in the social fold post-injury or post-retirement from the game. That's why you have heard and listened and even been advised to complete your academics while pursuing your game. You have been advised to pick some vocational training. These are necessary goods that you must pursue towards a dignified end. So, that you have a good life even after retirement.

There are delightful goods that we enjoy and are harmless. We pursue it at leisure. And we know it may not hurt us and affect us in the long run. Like you always wanted to own a Cherokee and go to college driving it. Of course, the desire to own one was because you wanted to and not because of peer pressure, and certainly not because you have to fit in some way. Lastly, there is the noble good that is honorable and righteous. It satisfies your senses and cleanses your soul.

In today's world, it's fashionable to attach value to everything. How can you differentiate between what is valuable and what is good? Both are practically the same thing. We value something if it's good. The good always has the essence of something valuable. Value is subjective and is internal depending on our cultural and moral conditioning. Good is objective and universal. What kind of goods we must inculcate in our lives to pursue a good life? If we have to give it names, then they are as follows:

a) Virtuous Good
b) Useful Good
c) Pleasant Good

What is virtuous is good in itself? It is right and desired for its own sake. You follow it because it's the path where there's no collision with the wrong or evil. The mere appetite that relatively ends after it has been fulfilled does not drive it. Pleasant good is not absolute like the virtuous good. It is always relative. It meets an end, then its novelty is gone. Pleasure seekers whom we call hedonists believe in just pursuing one goal all of their lives, and that is a pleasure. Do you think they're the happiest of all among us? Do you think they have a good life among us? The moment you idolize something, you destroy it. Pleasure is not something to idolize. Happiness is always in arriving at an end that's noble.

Happiness is never an end in itself. It's not like Roger Federer has ever thought of winning the highest number of Grand Slams equitable to absolute happiness in his life. He would have been happy while striving for it. Usain Bolt made the world record in 100 meters just because he wanted to be happy. Happiness is always the byproduct. Useful goods are like tools for achieving a virtuous good or a pleasant good. Useful goods are not utility in a utilitarian sense or a pragmatist sense. That it must be practical and useful and not relative to some absolute end these things are useful for.

Everyone complains that life is too complex these days. There're so many technological devices to manage the time that gives us a minute-to-minute update on our daily chores. It even gives us the biometric data that whether we are stressed or not while going about our work. We have become slaves to burgeoning technology. We have been slaves as a consumer for a while. We don't know we can simplify our lives by not just looking at things as a consumer to a disposable end. You want to have a simplified and unencumbered life? Follow the above-described goods by keeping them relative to the highest good that is God's good. It's written in the Bible that, "Do not withhold good from those whom it's due when it is in your power to act" (*NIV* Proverb 3:23).

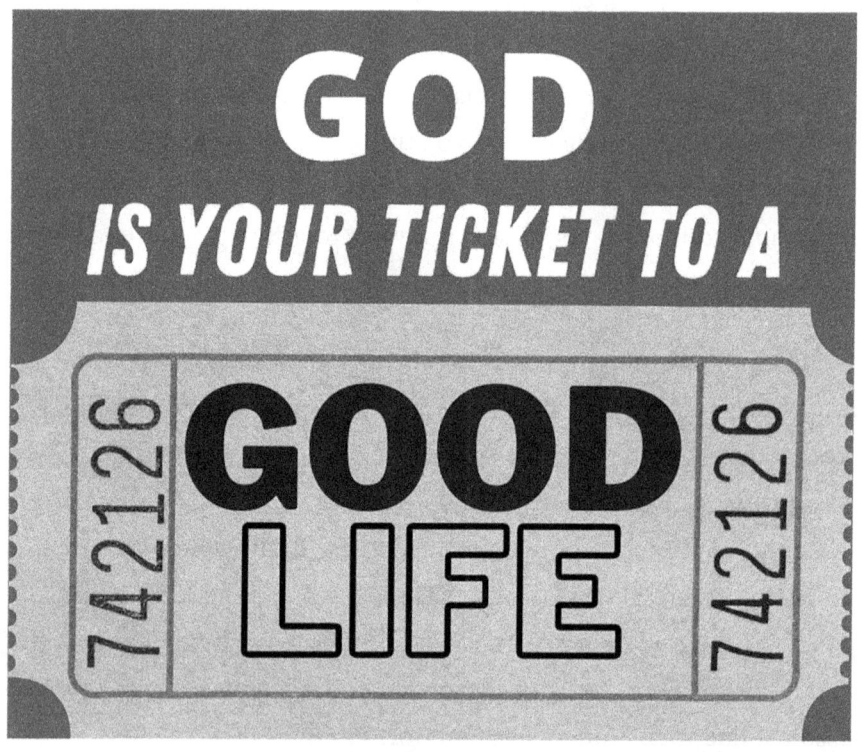

A good life is a beautiful life. What is beauty? Some find it in symmetry like everything that exists in nature has some kind of symmetry: a tree, a butterfly, a fallen leaf, the shape of celestial bodies, you wonder how come the full moon looks so perfect, some see it in the physical attributes of a soul, for some, it is an abstract and subjective principle. You can't comprehend it. It can come to you from any side if you keep your mind open to it. It is omniscient. It is perceived by our senses with the able help of our mind. For a physical thing, we look for the immensity of its beauty. It fills us with awe as if it overwhelms us. For a lover, it could be his beloved's collar bone. When you look at the Grand Canyon you're struck by something that's beyond your imagination but that has been in the making for years and years. We can similarly say about nature's phenomenon of Aurora Borealis. Beautiful objects are small. Beautiful objects are parts of a whole. And that immensity and wholeness is the Lord's grace and his divinity. A beautiful life is when it meets the desire of God. It's the state of happiness that satisfies us all together. It's the end that human will should seek. Nothing in the world would satisfy us except the universal good that is to be found not in any creature but God alone, because every creature has goodness by participation. Where God's goodness stands on its own and satisfies the human will. It's in the Bible that "Delight yourself in the Lord, and he will give you the desires of the heart" (*NIV*, Psalm 37:4). Therefore God alone constitutes man's happiness. It's the perfect happiness that consists of a good life.

So far we have been discussing life in general what goodness it should constitute. We still have to discuss an athlete's life. Athletes' lives are not similar to normal lives. Their joy and pain are different. Their hardships are on another level. The return and riches are equally pleasant. During their lives, they confront a wide range of issues: Social, emotional, psychological, and financial. We shall discuss the bad part of an athlete's life so that you could prepare for it beforehand. It's hard for an athlete to go back to their social lives when they were away from it, most of their lives toiling in the field or traveling. They never get the time to build their social selves. Hence they feel alienated when they go back. In most cases, they don't find anything to engage themselves with. In no time, if there's no social outreach program, they recede to alcoholism or other escape routes that are psychologically scarring for them.

It is the same when the athlete's contract is terminated for some reason or an injury has confined them to life where returning to the field is impossible. The situation is dire during the transition period. The athlete is aware of the fact that he is past his prime, his age is taking its toll on him, he will get a termination any time sooner, still, he remains ignorant of it.

It's like someone awaiting death. It is as horrific as it can get. Let's face the harsh truth. The management knows, your teammates know, your coach knows except you. The next stage comes when the coach gives you some hint. The third stage comes when you realize what is to come and you await your departure. The final stage is when you exit. And it's just the start. You have to kick start your life again. You have to imagine and learn the new realities of your life. You have to unlearn the old language and habits that came with the game that is like your second skin. But, you have to shed it. Now you have to substitute your activity in the ground with something that suits your current life.

Do you have any skills to get back to the labor force again? Do you have any skills that can be used in nurturing new talents? Does the state have any mechanism in place to get you back to the fold and make your transition or retirement bearable? We all know every sport has its subculture, where we interact with the same number of people for a longer period. An athlete becomes group-conscious in the process. He feels being left out when he is out of his core group. It's not easy to adjust to the change in environment and to adapt to the new social norms.

There's one thread that connects your active life as a sports person to ordinary life, and that thread is contentment. Again, it brings us to the point of value attachment. Were we contented when fortune took a liking to us, were we indifferent to the fame and material good in our heydays? Contentment comes from God. You won't find it hard in continuing with your new life.

You have honored what you have been given before; you will honor what you will get now. Now, from a social perspective, retirement is seen as some sort of disengagement from the active life. It comes after an age, relatively in the latter stage of life. When it comes to athletes, they are able to retire from active sports at a relatively younger age. If we bring gender dynamics into it, women athletes are eligible to retire even early than their male counterparts. So retirement from sports is different from the normal retirement where people get retired from some jobs. When an athlete goes back to the social fold, he gets judged the same as the people who get retired at an old age. That adjusts a little troublesome when an athlete gets labeled externally. Hence engagement is an absolute necessity. You must utilize your energy to the maximum return.

There are stages of grief and pain that an athlete goes through after it's over:

    a) Denial and Isolation: He doesn't accept his present situation or his deteriorating sports acumen. He avoids his teammates so as reality doesn't hit him in the face.
    b) Anger: Since an athlete can't do anything about it. He becomes angry and tries to lengthen his sporting career through negotiation, and sometimes he goes beyond what his dignity would have allowed him to save his career.
    c) Stress and depression: It happens when they can't get their heads around it, and that takes a mental toll.
    d) Acceptance: They eventually come to accept their present situation in their lives.

There are a few more variables that affect an athletes' overall being when bad things like termination, or an irrevocable injury happen. And that is:

    a) Psychosocial competence
    b) Sex, Gender
    c) Age, State of Health
    d) Race, Ethnicity
    e) Socioeconomic status

Some transitions happen when an athlete goes from junior to senior level, from amateur level to a professional level, from a regional level to a national level. These transitions register themselves as events that something tangible has happened in someone's career. These transitions are generally anticipated since you get hints from the management and coach alike.

The transition becomes a non-event when a sudden injury stops your transfer from junior level to senior level. You're out of the game for possibly two years. Here you don't anticipate your exit. It is unpredicted and involuntary. You don't participate in it. You're not prepared for it because of its sudden nature rearing its head at the strangest of times. That's why it's unsettling. That's why it's scary. It's the same when you're retiring from the game.

Sometimes an athlete withdraws himself from the game because of the non-satisfaction. He couldn't drive much meaning from his sporting life and just dropped out. Some talented athlete withdraws from the game because of the financial implications. Some withdraw from the game because of gender-related issues. Some withdraw from the game because they were not able to fulfill their psychological and emotional needs like spending time with family and friends. Voluntary retirement is easy to the point that you anticipate it, you know it. But, still, the process to get back to normal life is not easy.

The socialization process is important during the formative years of any athlete, how he has been culturally conditioned.

Does he have any social skills to form his social identity independent from his sporting identity? At an elite level, athletes seldom get time to develop his social identity that's why he feels inhibited when he leaves the ground or when he resumes any non-athletic role.

What kind of coping skills does an athlete have? Can he manage his internal demand and external demand because of the changing environment? These are important questions. Next thing is to manage the problem at hand because he has bills to pay. And most importantly, can he manage emotionally? Does an athlete have sound emotional backing, either from his family or his loved ones or from the neighborhood? We're talking about active social support here. There are athletes intervention program in place that is listed below:

Athlete career intervention programs

Program Country Organization

Athlete Career and Education Australia/UK Australian Institute of Sport/UK Sports (ACE)

Olympic Job Opportunities International, Ernst & Young Program (OJOP)

Olympic Athlete Career Centre Canada, Canadian Olympic Association (OACC)

Career Assistance Program, US United States Olympic Committee for Athletes (CAPA)

Making the Jump Program, US Advisory Resource Center for Athletes Women's Sports Foundation, US Women's Sports Foundation Athlete Service

Career Transition Program, US National Football League

CHAMPS/Life Skills, US National Collegiate Athletic Association

Making the Jump Program, US Springfield College

Study and Talent Education Belgium Free University of Brussels Program

The Retiring Athlete, The Netherlands Dutch Olympic Committee

The program has the motto of giving dignity to the athletes' life by identifying their transferable skills and employs them accordingly. The Ace program described above is to strike a balance in the athlete's life by providing him other skills like vocational training or fulfilling his academic needs.

If at the end of the chapter, we put a question forward that whether man's happiness consists of fame and glory? Happiness is what we strive for. Happiness is man's true good. Fame and glory are false. Glory means being well known and praised. It's the thing known to human knowledge. Fame and glory have existed in some form or other since time memorial. Alexander was the world conqueror. There was a time when the sun never set in the British Empire. Whereas God's knowledge is the cause of all things, He is the principal mover. If we're talking about absolute happiness here, then it's not possible with human knowledge. So, all the glory and praise are bestowed to him and him only.

A man's good which, through fame and glory, is in the knowledge of many, if this knowledge is true, and must be derived from the good existing in the man himself. And the good is God's good. Life is good and glorious when a man drives his glory from God.

If you want to hear more on Good Life, listen to Audio Adrenaline who asks us to appreciate the simple things in life that Lord has given to us:

The Greatest Teammate

Throw a blanket on the tailgate
Listen to the bullfrog serenade in the moonlight
In the truck bed dancin' slow
We'll sing along with the radio
Sippin' on grandma's homemade wine
Livin' the good life
Yeah, this is the good life
That's right (1999).

Thank you for taking the time to read this book. I hope you choose God as your teammate and hit a homerun in life.

Acknowledgments

This book would not have been possible without the influence and support of some amazing people that I have in my life. There are so many that I would like to give thanks to.

First and foremost, praises and thanks to God, the Almighty, for His blessings and His will throughout my career and my research, and for helping me complete the research successfully.

My wife, Jean, my best friend and my greatest support system—I am very much thankful for her love, patience, understanding, prayers, and continued support. She sets great examples for our children as a hardworking Christian wife and mother. There is no telling where I would be without her. She is my superhero.

My children, Drake, Drew, Madeleine, and Reese, my number-one team—I know I have made my share of mistakes as a parent, like every parent does, and I will probably make several more. However, the bond and relationship I have with my four children is irreplaceable. Through the many mental and physical training sessions, to the challenging life lessons we learned together, I couldn't be more proud and grateful to have these four as my number-one team.

The Greatest Teammate

My parents, Ava and Dean—I am blessed and grateful to have parents who guided me and laid the foundation of preparing me for life after sports. They were my biggest fans and number-one support system. I thank them for the countless hours they put in and the sacrifices they made during my youth years as a multi-sport athlete. Nevertheless, they never let me lose sight of my priority to grow up to be a hardworking, well-mannered, and disciplined Christian man.

My siblings—I express my thanks to my brother, Chris, and to my sisters, Angie and Diana, for their support throughout the years.

My Preachers and Youth Pastors- Charles Gilder, Paul Gilder, and Marty Harden.

Quint Studer, my mentor and inspiration—A special thank you to Quint Studer, owner of the Pensacola Blue Wahoos baseball team, who gave me my first job in professional baseball. His leadership and training helped me to become a better leader and gave me the ability to help others. His inspiration also helped me to become a better person, better husband, and better father. I credit much of my success to Quint as a mentor and a friend.

My coaches/mentors—These are coaches I played for and/or coaches I have worked with who have been positive influences in my life and who have helped pave my way to a successful career in sports while helping me keep my focus on the bigger picture. In no particular order, I would like to thank Mike Aloisio, Lud Henry, John Skelton, Tim Hymel, Oliver Winston, Cooper Farris, Rick Rhodes, Dave Saunders, Bill Hamilton, Doug Martin, Ryan Antoine, and Tommy Minton.

My current and former players—Thank you to my players who put their trust and faith in me as their baseball coach, sport psychology coach, personal trainer, and college placement consultant. Everyone who makes baseball great—Thank you to all the players, coaches (volunteers and hired coaches alike), parents, umpires, and others who devote their time and passion to sports.

John Melvin Publishing—This company is named in honor of my late brother-in-law, a great athlete whom I had the honor of coaching many years ago. John, you are loved and missed.

Other Books by David L. Angeron

David Angeron
THE CHALLENGING ROAD TO SUCCESS: A Guided Road Map to Quality Mental, Physical, and Spiritual Habits for Your Journey to Success
★★★★★ (5)

David Angeron
THE MENTAL TRAINING GUIDE FOR ELITE ATHLETES: How the Mental Master Method Helps Players, Parents, and Coaches Create a Championship Mindset
★★★★★ (32)

David Angeron
IT'S MY TIME: Understanding College Recruiting and College Placement
★★★★☆ (5)

REFERENCES

Adrenaline, A. (1999). Underdog, Prod. Charlie Peacock.

Aquinas, T. (1265-1274). Summa Theologica, Of the Gift of Fortitude. Christian Classics, Ethereal Library. (P. 4012-4014)

Aquinas, T. (1265-1274). Summa Theologica, Whether Confidence Belongs to Magnanimity Christian Classics, Ethereal Library (P. 3946-3952).

Aquinas, T. (1265-1274). Summa Theologica; Of Prayer. Christian Classics, Ethereal Library (P. 3489-3522).

Aquinas, T. (1265-1274). Summa Theologica; Of the Image. Christian Classics, Ethereal Library.

Aquinas, T. (1265-1274). Summa Theologica; Of the necessity of grace? Christian Classics, Ethereal Library (P.2526-2529).

Aquinas, T. (1265-1274). Summa Theologica; Of The Will of God. Christian Classics, Ethereal Library (P.237-240).

Aquinas, T. (1265-1274). Summa Theologica; Those Things that are Required for Happiness. Christian Classics, Ethereal Library (P.1345-1376).

Aquinas, T. (1265-1274). Summa Theologica; whether doubts should be interpreted for the best? Christian Classics, Ethereal Library (P.3283-3285).

Aquinas, T. (1965). Thomism, The Philosophy of Thomas Aquinas, Love and the Passions & The Personal Life, Etienne Gilson, Trans. Laurence K. Shook & Armand Maurer, Edit. Sixth, Pontifical Institute of Medieval studies (309-345).

Aquinas, T. (1965). Thomism, The Philosophy of Thomas Aquinas, The Religious Life, Etienne Gilson, Trans. Laurence K. Shook & Armand Maurer, Edit. Sixth, Pontifical Institute of Medieval studies.

Aquinas, T. (1965). Thomism, The Philosophy of Thomas Aquinas; The Nature of Thomistic Philosophy, Etienne Gilson, Trans. Laurence K. Shook & Armand Maurer, Edit. Sixth, Pontifical Institute of Medieval studies (P.1-27).

Aquinas, T. (1965). Thomism, The Philosophy of Thomas Aquinas; The Religious Life, Etienne Gilson, Trans. Laurence K. Shook & Armand Maurer, Edit. Sixth, Pontifical Institute of Medieval studies.

Aristotle. (2011). Nicomachean Ethics, Book 1, Book 3, Book 4, Book 5, and Book 10, Trans. Robert C, Bartlett & Susan D. Collins, The University of Chicago Press.

Augustine, St. (1998). Confessions. Trans. Henry Chadwick, Oxford University Press.

Augustine, St. (1998). Confessions. Trans. Henry Chadwick, Oxford University Press.

Augustine, St. (1998). Confessions. Trans. Henry Chadwick, Oxford University Press.

Augustine, St. (1998). Confessions; Book 3, Book 4, & Book 5, Trans. Henry Chadwick, Oxford University Press (P.57-100).

Augustine, St. (1998). Confessions; Finding the Church in Genesis 1, Book 13, Trans. Henry Chadwick, Oxford University Press (P.262-287).

Augustine, St. (1998). Confessions; Memory, Book 1 to Book 7, Trans. Henry Chadwick, Oxford University Press (P.29-140).

Augustine, St. (1998). Confessions; Memory, Book 10, Trans. Henry Chadwick, Oxford University Press (P.181-214).

Augustine, St. (1998). Confessions; Memory, Book 10, Trans. Henry Chadwick, Oxford University Press (P181-214).

Augustine, St. (1998). Confessions; Time and Eternity, Book 11, Trans. Henry Chadwick, Oxford University Press (P.217-236).

Barton C, S. (2000). The Challenges of Jesus' Parables; Parable on God's Love and Forgiveness, Edit. Richard N. Longenecker, Wm. B. Eerdmans Publishing Co. (P.199-215)

Bunyan, J. (2008). Pilgrim's Progress. The Project Gutenberg E-Text.

Burke, E. (1998). The Philosophical Inquiry; The Real Cause of Beauty. Edit. Adam Phillips, Oxford World Classics (P.102).

Burton, D & Raedeke D, T. (2008). Sport Psychology for Coaches, Human Kinetics (P. 52-64).

Crowns, Casting. (2003). Voice of Truth, Prod. Steven Curtis Chapmas & Mark Miller.

Crowns, Casting. (2005). Praise you in this Storm, Prod. Mark Miller.

Crowns, Casting. (2013). Courageous, Prod. Mark Miller.

Eklund C, R. & Tenenbaum, G. (2014). Encyclopedia of Sports Psychology. Sage Publications.

Fagothey, A Fr. (1959). Right and reason: Ethics based on the Teachings of Aristotle and Thomas Aquinas; The Good. The C.V. Mosby Cmpany (P.22-24).

Flame. (2013). Royal Flush, Starting Over, Track 15, Prod. Justin Ebach.

France T, R. (2000). The Challenges of Jesus' Parables. On Being ready. Edit. Richard N. Longenecker, Wm. B. Eerdmans Publishing Co. (P. 177-195)

Funk W, R., Hoover W, R., & The Jesus Seminar. (1997). The Five Gospels; The Search for the Authentic Words of Jesus; The Gospel of Mark, Harper Collins Publishers (P. 39-129).

Funk W, R., Hoover W, R., and The Jesus Seminar. (1997). The Five Gospels; The Search for the Authentic Words of Jesus; The Gospel of Matthew, Harper Collins Publishers. (P. 129 -270)

God is Enough. (2010). Lecrae, Rehab. Prod. Pete Kipley.

Haht N, T. (1987). The Miracle of Mindfulness; One is all, All is one: The five Aggregators, Trans. Moby Ho, Beacon Press (P. 45-55).

Holder, A. (2005). The Blackwell Companion to Christian Spirituality. Blackwell Publishing.

I Can only Image. (1999). Mercy Me, The Worship project. Prod. Pete Kipley.

James, W. (1890). The Principles of Psychology, The Consciousness of self, Dover Edition. (P.291-305)

Kenneson, P. (2004). The Blackwell Companion to Christian Ethics; Gathering: Worship, Imagination, and Formation. Edit. Stanley Hauerwas & et al;. Blackwell Publishing (P.54-67).

Kreeft, P. (2014). Practical Theology; Only Three Kinds of Goods. Ignatius Press (P.47-48).

Lavallee, D; Kremer, J; Moran P, A; Williams, M. (2004). Sport Psychology, Anxiety. Palgrave Macmillan. (P. 118-138)

Lavallee, D; Kremer, J; Moran P, A; Williams, M. (2004). Sport Psychology, Exercise and Mental Health. Palgrave Macmillan. (P. 233-256)

Lavallee, D; Kremer, J; Moran P, A; Williams, M. (2004). Sport Psychology, Imagery. Palgrave Macmillan.

Lavallee, D; Kremer, J; Moran P, A; Williams, M. (2004). Sport Psychology, Teams. Palgrave Macmillan (P.182-207).

Mills W, C. (2007). Baseball Superstars; Derek Jeter, Chelsea House Publishers (P 1- 98).

Move. (2010). Flame, Captured.

Pascal, B. (1910). Thoughts, Letters, and Minor Works. Trans. W.F. Trotter, M.L.Booth, O.W.Wight. The Harvard Classics, Collier and Sons.

Roush, Sherrilyn, "Epistemic Self-Doubt", The Stanford Encyclopedia of Philosophy (Winter 2017 Edition), Edward N. Zalta (ed.), URL = <https://plato.stanford.edu/archives/win2017/entries/epistemic-self-doubt/>. Accessed on 15/12/2020.

Russell J, R. (2005). The Blackwell Companion to Christian Spirituality, Natural Sciences. Edit. Arthur Holder, Blackwell Publishing. (P. 325-340)

Sartre J, P. (1989). No Exit & Three Other Plays, Vintage International, (P.1-46)

Seneca. (2007). Dialogues and Essays, Trans. John Davie, Oxford University Press.

Seneca. (2010). Selected Letters, Trans. Elaine Fantham, Oxford University Press.

Spinoza, B. (2002). Complete Works; Short Treatise on God, Man, and His Well-Being. Trans. Samuel Shirley, Edit. Michael L. Morgan, Hackett Publishing Company, Inc. (P.31-108).

The Bible, American Standard Version, https://www.biblegateway.com, accessed on. 9/12/2020.

The Bible, Douay-Rheims 1899 American Edition, DRA, https://www.biblegateway.com, accessed on. 1/02/2021.

The Bible, English Standard Version, ESV https://www.biblegateway.com, accessed on. 1/02/2021.

The Bible, Living Bible, TLB https://www.biblegateway.com, accessed on. 5/02/2021.

The Bible, New International Version, NIV https://www.biblegateway.com, accessed on. 5/02/2021.

The Bible, New King James Version, https://www.biblegateway.com, accessed on. 15/12/2020.

The Bible, NEW LIVING TRANSLATION, NLT, https://www.biblegateway.com, accessed on. 22/03/2021.

The Bible, New Revised Standard Version, NRSV https://www.biblegateway.com, accessed on. 5/02/2021.

The Holy Bible, Christian Standard Bible, https://www.biblegateway.com, accessed on. 3/12/20.

The Holy Bible, English Standard Version, https://www.biblegateway.com, accessed on. 1/04/20.

The Holy Bible, Living Bible, https://www.biblegateway.com, accessed on. 18/12/20.

The Holy Bible, New International Version, https://www.biblegateway.com, accessed on. 1/04/20.

The Holy Bible, New King James Version, https://www.biblegateway.com, accessed on. 18/12/20.

The Holy Bible, World English Bible, https://www.biblegateway.com, accessed on. 3/12/20.

Torrell J, P. (2011). Christ and Spirituality in St. Thomas Aquinas; Charity as Ffriendship & The Image of Christ as the Preacher, Trans. Bernhard Blankenhorn, The catholic University of American Press (P.45-173).

Torrell J, P. (2011). Christ and Spirituality in St. Thomas Aquinas; Christ in the Spirituality of St. Thomas, Trans. Bernhard Blankenhorn, The catholic University of American Press (P.74-109).

Vanhoozer J, K. (2004). The Blackwell Companion to Christian Ethics. Edit. Stanley Hauerwas & et al; Blackwell Publishing.

Vealey S, R. (2007). Handbook of Sports Psychology, Mental skills Training in Sport. Edit. Robert C. Eklund and Gershon Tenenbaum. John Wiley & Sons, Inc. (P. 287-301)

Weil, S. (1973). Waiting for God. Trans. Emma Crawford, Harper & Row Publishers.

Weil, S. (1978). Lectures on Philosophy, Courage. Trans. Hugh Price, Cambridge University Press. (P. 210)

Weil, S. (2002). Gravity and Grace, To Desire Without an Object, Trans. Emma Crawford, Routledge Classics (P.22-25).

Weil, S. (2002). Gravity and Grace; The Self, Trans. Emma Crawford, Routledge Classics (P.26-31).

Weil, S. (2003). Gravity and Grace. Trans. Emma Crawford, Routledge Classics.

Weirzbicka, A. (2001). What Did Jesus Mean; Explaining the Sermon on the Mount and the Parables in Simple and Universal Human Concepts, Parables, Oxford University Press.

You Can't Stop Me. (2014). Andy Mineo, Never Land. Prod. Alex Medina.

www.ingramcontent.com/pod-product-compliance
Lightning Source LLC
Chambersburg PA
CBHW071855160426
43209CB00005B/1070